Ghost No More

~ a memoir ~

CeeCee James

DEDICATION

~ To my family, my answered prayers 333 ~

CONTENTS

~ Introduction ~

This is my journey back from fear and hopelessness, and how I went from feeling like a ghost, to realizing my voice and value. I own it and share it because it has no power over me anymore.

I've written my story as accurately as my memory would allow. The names and locations have been changed to protect the people in my memoir. My story isn't about assigning blame, or making people out to be villains.

There is light at the end of the tunnel. You, the reader, are amazing. You are a gift. Your identity isn't what someone has ever said about you. Your identity isn't how you think you compare with someone else, or how you think you could be better. You're made for good things, deeply loved, talented, and valuable. And you deserve love.

I once hated my past. It had broken and twisted me, but now I appreciate all the beauty and redemption God has brought from each broken area.

Taking a big breath now, here is my story.

~ 1 ~
TURNING INVISIBLE

"You know, CeeCee," Mama said, not looking up at me, "I was lost in the desert once."

I froze, afraid to move a muscle. I didn't want to break the spell causing Mama to talk to me. They were her first words to me in two days.

Mama sat on the floor staring at a picture in her lap-- a picture that Grandma had painted of Arizona. She lit a cigarette, paused to take a deep drag, her eyes focused on the yellow painting.

"Your dad and I were in the Sonoran desert looking for peyote when I was pregnant with you. And then the car died. I told your Dad that car was a pile of crap, but he never listened to me." "He had this great idea to take a short cut back to town." She snorted and shook her head. "Instead, we were lost for hours. I thought we'd die out there."

She jerked her head up and gave me a sharp look, and my eleven-year-old heart jumped. "Somehow, we found our way back. I remember thinking I was never going to get away from him, because of you. I ended up going into labor, and your dad left me alone at the hospital on his way to the bar to get drunk."

She stood to put the painting back in the box.

"Mama, were you happy? You know, when I was born." I blurted out before she could turn her back, and the moment was gone forever.

"You were a terrible baby, just screamed all day. But I didn't let you manipulate me with your crying." Her lip showed a hint of a smile as she remembered. "I use to let you scream until your face turned black. I kept the bedroom door closed and let your dad deal with you when he got home."

She paused from folding the tissue paper around the painting and turned with a dark sneer. "Don't think he's a good guy. Your dad destroyed your baby book one night when he was drunk."

She abruptly left the room, returning a minute later with a white photo album that she set before me on the kitchen counter. I looked at her for a second and then opened the book. The first picture captured Mama in 1973. She was twenty, beautiful, and smiling with the confidence of a woman who once had every football player at her high school chase after her. I was perched on her lap, and Mama's hands were tucked under her legs to avoid touching me. Another picture caught her in mid-laugh. She was with Dad and his older cousin, her arm coquettishly wrapped around the cousin.

The next page had photos of me as a toddler proudly being displayed in front of my grandparents' fruit trees, flowers, and their house, and in each picture I was wearing a variation of plaid pants and a long sleeve shirt.

"Why am I wearing long sleeves in the summer?" I asked.

"To hide the bruises. Your dad wore so many rings. Your Grandpa threatened to call CPS on him all the time."

I hesitated for a moment, before tapping on the picture of my second birthday. "Why do I have a black eye?"

"Oh, I popped you one that morning because you were being smart to me. Now go outside."

I had an assignment at school the next week to bring in baby pictures. I cut some out of a magazine and pasted those to my project instead.

***

When I was two, my parents and I lived in a farmhouse in Pennsylvania. The house was big and white, with a muddy yard in front, and two garages that jutted out on the side where Dad ran his motorcycle business.

Nearly every morning, as soon as I finished my breakfast that Dad set out for me, I ran outside. He was already out there, working on one bike or another. I was scared to be in the farmhouse alone. The house was hollow and cold; and the wooden floor gave sharp creaks that made my skin prickle. Mama stayed in one of the rooms upstairs. I knew better than to go look for her.

Outside, I sang, "la, la, la, la," and used my shovel to fill my blue plastic wheelbarrow with dirt. I had made a path in the golden grass that led between the two garages. I thought for the most part that life was silent, ants were silent, grass was silent, and my parents were silent. The only sound was my own voice.

There was always a parade of motorcycles lined up in the sun, waiting for Dad to fix them. I pushed my wheelbarrow past them and dumped the dirt at the end, jumping up and down on it to pound the dirt flat. I looked at the motorcycles and squinted. The chrome trim flashed back the reflection of the sun and hurt my eyes. Near one of the bike tires was a pile of gasoline-soaked rags. I loved the smell of gas and crouched over them to smell them. Dad yelled from the garage, "Get away from there!"

Dad saw me! As fast as I could, I ran from the rags into the muddy yard, almost tripping on the rope that tied our dog, Bo, to a rotting dog house. He looked at me with sad eyes. I put my arms around him, my face burying in the fur of his dirty neck and squeezed him tight. He made a quick snarl and bit my arm. I shoved him away with a scream, hurt and anger pumping through my lungs. Mama came out onto the porch with her cigarette and poked it in my direction, "Serves you right for messing with him."

It was the first time I saw her since the night before.

Mama liked to be left alone. Whenever I caught her eye in the house, she'd point her finger to the front door, "Out."

She was also rough if she had to touch me. My stomach felt like I had swallowed rocks if I heard her come down the hall in the morning to help me dress for the day. She'd whip the pants out of the drawer with a dark look on her face and jam my legs into the holes. Then she'd lift me up by the band of the pants and shake me until I slid into them like a pillow in a pillow case. I learned to suck in my stomach because she snapped them quick, more than once catching my skin.

After she pulled the shirt over my head, I'd scramble to get my own arms through the sleeve holes. I didn't like having her hands under my shirt with her sharp nails, where there was grabbing and twisting to get my hands through the sleeves.

Mama didn't like to be around Dad either. One night, I was

woken up by a loud cry that came from downstairs. A minute later there was a scream that was abruptly cut off. The hair on the back of my neck stood up as I rolled out of bed. I tip-toed out of my room because the plastic bottoms of my pajama feet scratched on the wood floor. With my blanket wrapped over my arm, I snuck part way down the stairs to peek through the railing.

It was bright in the kitchen. Dad was walking behind Mama who sat at the table. His eyes glared with anger, but she wouldn't look at him. He slapped the table next to her, and both she and I jumped at the sound. When he walked behind her, she whimpered, and his lips curled in a snarl. He slapped her with a crack that made me yelp, but I was drowned out by her scream.

I stuffed my blanket in my mouth and curled down on the step. I didn't know adults hit each other; I thought they only hit children. When Mama quit crying, I peeked out one more time and then crept back up the stairs to my room. I squished my eyes tight, trying to stop the image from replaying in the darkness.

It wasn't long after that night when Dad caught me sneaking a piece of candy from my Easter basket. He raised his hand. I flinched and stumbled back. I was afraid of the big ring on Dad's left hand. The blue stone in it winked evilly at me. But, he pointed toward the dark, wood-paneled corner. He had me stand there while he leaned back in a chair and watched me like a cat watches a mouse. With a singsong tone, he directed me, "Stand up. Sit down. Stand up. Sit down. Stand up. Sit down." He sipped from his coffee cup and ate my candy while he watched my legs shake. It lasted for hours, until he grew bored and my candy was gone. My nose slid up and down a black groove in the paneling, and I wished there was an escape.

My third birthday was a few days later. Dad called me to get on his bike. He strapped the white helmet on to my head, and thumped the top twice, "There you go, mushroom head." He grinned and picked me up, setting me on the black seat, and then climbed on in front of me. Mom rode behind me. My arms weren't able to reach around Dad, so I clutched the stiff leather of his jacket at his sides, and my hands ached from the effort. I cried every time I rode behind him, afraid I might let go and fall off onto the rushing blurred pavement. Mama always said, "I'm just waiting for your laces to be eaten up by that engine!"

We roared up to Grandma's house. Dad climbed off, leaving me to scramble down on my own. He walked into Grandma's house before us. Mama pulled me back with a jerk on my arm and said, "If you embarrass me, I'll give you a smack you won't forget," before she shoved me into the house. The kitchen was filled with my relatives. I winked back tears. Grandma clapped, and I ran over to hug her knees.

There was cheering so I tried to smile back. My cousins batted balloons back and forth over my head. I watched them and thought the balloons floated by magic.

Grandma gave me a plastic tea-set with a big red ribbon. I felt a splat as my cousin stuck the bow to the top of my head, which made me laugh, until the tape pulled my hair when I tried to yank it off. Someone opened the tea-set package for me, and I set the cups on the tiny plates around the table. Humming, I poured a cup with my plastic teapot. My cousin grabbed at the teapot.

"It's mine! Grandma gave it to me!" I said.

Mama pinched me hard on the underside of my arm and hissed under her breath, "You share that toy with your cousin."

I handed the teapot over to my cousin with a lump in my throat. Mama thought I wasn't a nice girl, like my cousin Christy. "Smile!" There was a flash as Grandma took a picture.

Later, I went outside to have a few minutes by myself. My first prayer came as I walked around on the top of an old railroad tie that edged the garden. My three-year-old self reached out to the Creator, and I prayed over and over in a chant, "Please God, let me start over. Let me start my life over. I will be good this time. I will do it right. I will be a good girl. I will be good."

~ 2 ~
THE ESCAPE

The summer of 1976, when I was three, Mama packed me in her old Pontiac, along with a few grocery bags of clothes, and we left our white farm house. I sat in the back seat of Mama's car. Her eyes flashed angrily when they caught mine in the rear-view mirror.

"Your Dad threatened to hunt me down and kill me if I left him," she blurted out. I looked at her wide eyed. "He's looking for us right now. I stayed with him all these years because of you."

I slid my fingers along the stitching on the green vinyl back seat as heat flooded my face. Slowly, I scooted my body out of reach from a back slap of her hand. My nose still hurt from the one earlier. I didn't know how mad she was, and didn't know what to say to make it better.

"Sorry Mama," I whispered.

Mama stepped on the gas and I lurched back into the seat. "He's a sadist!" I had no idea what that was, but nodded and listened with my thumb in my mouth. My other hand tried to twirl a short wisp of my hair. "I'll never forgive myself for what I allowed him to do to our pets. He killed every animal we owned."

Mama then described the time our mama cat had her kittens. When they were a few weeks old, Dad took the kittens upstairs to the bathroom. He filled the bath tub up with water, and then pushed the kittens beneath the surface of the water. He didn't let them drown straight away; he brought them back up to the surface to get a weak gasp of air. They meowed, before they sunk under the water again. If

6

Mama couldn't save the kittens, she probably couldn't save herself or me either.

As we drove I thought about our dog, Bo. I wondered if Dad killed him too, and pictured a cartoon dog ghost coming out of him, playing a harp while floating up to the clouds. I wriggled on the seat, tired of sitting. My legs were numb, was I ever going to get out? We had been in the car all day. Finally Mama turned off the highway and on to a country road. Where were we going? After a few more minutes Mama drove down a long, dusty driveway full of cars that led to a large brown house. The windows were opened and billowing checkered curtains waved at us when the breeze came through. A covered, painted porch with broad steps led to the front door, with white rocking chairs scattered between the open windows. The house itself was backed up against a green haze of woods.

We walked up the steps and Mama cleared her throat and took a deep breath before she pulled the wooden screen door open with a squeak. I stumbled over one of my blue tennis shoes that had come untied. I glanced down and saw my legs were grubby from playing outside earlier that morning. Tears stung my eyes. I didn't want anyone to see me looking like a dirty girl. Mama pushed me ahead of her into their living room. I wanted to hide behind her, but, she held me in front of her with a firm grip on my shoulder as the group of laughing people turned to look at us.

Their family was getting together that day for their annual barbeque, and Mama and I had been invited. The sea of strange faces left me frozen and bewildered, and unsure of how to act.

A teenage girl rescued me by bringing over a coloring book. She opened a new box of crayons, rows of colors, all with sharp points. I put my fingers in my mouth and glanced at Mama. Was I bothering the girl? But Mama had left the room. I took one of the crayons being held out to me and sat on the floor to color the princess picture. The teenage girl looked like the princess in the fairy tale coloring book, and I wanted to color the picture extra nice for her.

I watched their family while I colored. Boys chased each other around the couches and jumped over the coffee tables. Kids and the adults talked in happy and loud voices, but the words sounded jumbled to my ears. I blinked my eyes, glanced down and saw marks on the outside of the dark lines. I had ruined it.

One little girl with brown pigtails ran up to me and tried to catch my hand. She coaxed me to join her in the chasing, but I pulled my hand back. What does she want? She shrugged her shoulders and darted away to join a group of big girls, about six or seven years old. The girls held each other's hands in a long chain and raced outside, their bare feet slapping against the wood floor. Curious, I put down the crayon, and followed them, attracted to their pixie-like energy.

I approached their group with slow steps, but when the girls saw me draw near they bowled me over like a bunch of puppies. Their high-pitched chatter made me laugh. I let them grab my hands, and we ran, all linked together, down to the little pond at the edge of the property. I slipped off my shoes, and waded into the pond to try to catch the tiny, speckled gray minnows. The minnows were too fast for us, and darted away from our clumsy hands, only to tease us a moment later when they swam near our feet again. After a while we gave up chasing them, and instead played tag in the water. The thick mud squishing up between my toes made me giggle.

The sun was an orange ribbon rippling on the top of the water when the oldest cousin said, "It's time to bring Nana back the frogs." We shrieked and pointed whenever we saw the bulgy eyes of a frog peep up out of the water, and scrambled to catch it. I was excited to scream; there was no one to yell at me.

We brought back the frogs in the clear plastic containers, and an old woman met us at the back door. She thanked us while she wiped her hands on an apron.

"I'm going to cook up these here frogs," she said as the frogs hopped and thumped in the containers in her hands. We peeked through the kitchen door to watch, squealed at the thud of her knife, and ran away.

After dinner was over, Mama found me. I said goodbye but I didn't want to go. She walked ahead of me, tall tan legs-- she had a scab on the back of one-- and we climbed in her old junker car. As soon as we left the driveway she spoke.

"I don't like you talking to those people. They're my friends, not yours. I want you to stay out of sight. Next time walk away."

"Okay Mama."

We drove for a long time. My eyes felt heavy watching the tall trees fly by. I yawned. Much later, when it was dark, we drove back up that long dusty driveway with our headlights off. Mama stared at the dark house for a minute, and beckoned to me. I crawled out her side of the car, before she closed the door with a quiet click. We snuck onto the covered porch of the summer house. Mama, barely breathing, whispered to me.

"Quiet, be very quiet."

We climbed in the creaking rocking chairs. We slept on those chairs, and crept off when the sky became light gray the next day. The family didn't realize we were there at night. I thought it was an adventure and was too young to realize that we were homeless.

~ 3 ~
GRANDMA'S HOUSE

The next day, Mama called her old high school friend, her voice sounding higher-pitched than usual. They laughed and chatted over the phone, ending with an invite for us to stay with her until Mama was able to get back on her feet. When we pulled up outside the friend's house, Mama told me to stay in my room while we were there.

"She isn't used to kids. Don't talk to her and keep out of sight." I never saw either of them. I sat by the window in the bare white room and looked out, wishing I could play outside.

Mama got a job at an auto parts store, and woke me early each morning to drop me off at my paternal grandparents' house on her way to work. It was always silent in the car, Mama even kept the radio off.

I ate breakfast at my grandparent's house, picking a miniature box of cereal from a cellophane pack Grandma kept on the counter. Afterwards, I helped Grandma do the laundry in the basement. The basement was a maze of replaced kitchen counters, weight benches, painting supplies, and a corner filled with old dolls with little holes on their hairless heads and Hasbro games. She dragged a laundry basket across the cement basement floor to the washing machine. I hauled the warm clothes out of the dryer. The static snapped, and I laughed at the socks clinging to the shirts and dresses.

When the chores were done, Grandma gave me a powdered sugar cookie out of the yellow plastic container on the kitchen counter. We went into the living room and Grandma scooped me up to sit on her lap in the rocking chair. She wrapped her arms around me so that she could knit, her blue needles saying, "Clack. Clack. Clack."

Grandma's lips moved too, in little whispers.

"What Grandma?" I asked.

She smiled, "Let me count, CeeCee. This sweater is for your fourth birthday."

I heard a car pull up into the driveway and honk the horn. Mama sat out there, her car idling, so I kissed Grandma goodbye and ran outside.

***

One weekend, Mama and I went to an outdoor music concert with her older brother. It was hot and crowded as we drove around a dusty parking lot while Mama searched for an empty parking spot. Mama was tense when she caught my eye in the rear view mirror. "What did you say?" Her eyes narrowed into slits. I looked up at her in surprise. I hadn't said anything and started shaking my head in denial, but she still reached back and smacked me across the face. I held my swollen lip and hung my head, tasting blood. My uncle saw Mama's slap. He thought I was a bad girl too.

We got out of the car and found an empty spot in the grass among the crowds of people. The music started, and cheers began. Hands cupped around screaming mouths. I put my hands to my mouth and hooted through them too, squinting at the stage that was far away. That's the big deal? I could barely see the people, but the music was loud. People scrambled to their feet and began to jump and sway, pressing into me. My face smashed against someone's hip. I shoved back, my skinny arms pushing against the big adult bodies.

"Get away from me, you're squashing me," I yelled. Nobody listened.

Their moving bodies began to pinch me away from Mama. But, the further away I got from the stage, the more space there was. I wandered through the maze of people lying on blankets. The smell of the hot dogs and cookies reminded me that I was hungry. I rubbed my tummy near one kind-looking lady, hoping she would offer me some of the food scattered around her. A package of cookies had fallen to the side of a blanket and was half on the grass. My mouth watered, and I wiped it with the back of my hand. I'm a fast runner!

I started to reach out, but stopped. What if Mama sees me? A flash of fear zipped through me. I didn't know where Mama was. I spun around and felt dizzy. Everyone looked the same--- tan faces, and long hair, groups of screaming kids chasing each other in zig zags. A man, chugging a brown beer bottle pointed up to the sky, bumped into me. He hurt my foot. I cried, and limped away.

I searched all day before I found Mama. She was just standing up from the grass, brushing off her bottom. I ran up and whispered in her ear. She frowned at me, upset, because I had to go to the bathroom. She shook her head.

"I don't know where to find one," she said.

Mama tried to coax me to pee behind a tree but I was embarrassed with all the people crowding near. One freckle-faced boy cried "Boo!" from behind the tree that she wanted me to use.

"I can wait," I said. We left the parking lot, and my stomach growled.

That summer, the county fair was in town too. A few weeks had passed since the concert, and Mama had saved up enough money to take me and my uncle to the fair rides. They walked ahead of me, laughing, while I trailed behind them, careful to keep an eye on Mama's brown sandals---I didn't want to lose her again. We stood together in the hot sun in front of a little booth while they bought tickets.

After they bought them, Mama looked down at me. "You're not big enough, so only uncle and I are going. Sit here, and wait for us."

She pointed to a tuft of dead, yellow grass. My heart was heavy when she walked away. She's going to leave me again? The grass was stiff, and I scuffed my sneaker toe against it. I kicked the same clump over and over, breaking the grass off until only a stiff brush poked out of the ground.

I looked over at the bright colored carousel. There was a long line of children waiting their turn, holding sweaty tickets in their hands. The music rang like little bells. I wanted to be on one of the pretty horses going up and down. I tapped my feet, dancing to the ringing bells. The excitement caught me. I tapped harder and faster, spinning in my dance, my arms waving like snakes. I wanted one of the moms or dads standing in line to see me and think I was cute. Maybe they will offer me a ticket, I thought as I spun around. No one was looking at me, so I danced harder- tap, tap, tap- the scrubbed grass smashing into nothing under my feet. I did my big finish, TaDAAA!, my hands stretched wide, and then dipped into a curtsey. I panted, waiting for the reaction. The mothers and fathers were taking pictures of their kids going up and down on the horse, doing nothing special. The music went on, and the blinking lights went around. I sat down on the scrubbed-out grass and waited for Mama.

Several hours passed. The light was turning gray over the setting sun, when Mama and Uncle came back. They were laughing together, and he was talking about how there must be a lot of money on the ground from the people being spun upside down. Immediately, I studied the ground, hoping to see the flash of silver money sparkling up at me. I'm going to strike it rich! Maybe I can buy her a new home! Mama will give me a big hug! She told me to hurry to the car. I didn't want to get spanked, so I ran after her, leaving my riches behind for another girl to find.

~ 4 ~
THE APARTMENT

By the end of the summer Mama and I had moved into an apartment. The apartment building was tall, with huge, fat-leafed maple trees that lined the street. I knew we secretly lived on Sesame Street, and watched for Oscar to pop out of the trash can near the alley every time I walked up the steps to the apartment door. When I didn't see him, I thought, Wow! He really is grumpy. Mama parked the Pontiac out in front, right next to a permanent giant mud puddle that I jumped over to get to the sidewalk. Every day I studied the side of the building and tried to find my window. They all gave the same blank reflection of the gray sky.

The first time we had walked into the apartment Mama laid the keys on the counter with a clatter and said, "Kids stay in their rooms. This is my side. Stay there, unless I call you."

My room was my whole world. I stacked my blocks in the window sill and watched the street. There was a man who walked by every day, but he never looked up. One day, I tapped the window softly to see if he'd notice-- I didn't want Mama to hear-- still he hurried by. I saw my head bobbing in the window, and pulled my lips and stretched my cheeks into funny faces with my fingers. I accidentally touched the white of my eye and studied my reflection while I did it again. It doesn't hurt! I thought to myself, amazed. I must have special eyes.

When I was around Mama, she didn't talk. I also noticed she wouldn't look at me anymore. I even tipped my head down once to get her to see me, but she only turned her head to the left, and stared into the kitchen. "CeeCee, go in your room."

Days went by without her saying more than a couple words to me. I started to tip-toe when I left my room. Our house was very quiet, and I felt ghost-like as I tried to stay out of her sight.

One morning, Mama rushed past while I was at the table and told me to hurry and eat breakfast. I had just put a scoop of sugar on my Toastie O's and frowned when the sugar disappeared to the bottom of the cereal bowl. I ate as fast as I could, scraping the sugar up with my spoon, feeling it crunch in my mouth.

"CeeCee, we have to leave now!" I tipped the bowl back and drank the milk and then put the bowl in the sink.

Mama drove me to a long red building.

"This is preschool," she said, while filling out a piece of paper. She handed it to the lady and turned to look out the glass door at her car.

"Be good. I'll be back soon."

I watched her walk out the door, and ran after her.

"Don't go Mama!" I cried, but she didn't look back. The door shut, and she climbed in her car.

A woman with curly brown hair walked up to me. Her shoes were loud on the linoleum. I stopped crying to stare at them; funny, square-toed shoes that matched the brown color of her hair. She bent down.

"Welcome CeeCee. I'm the principal. Let's go into the gym where there are lots of fun games to play."

I liked that she bent down so that I could see her at eye-level. The gym was dark, with only half of the lights on. There were bouncy balls with handles, and I ran over to one and sat on it.

***

When I turned four, the principal bought me a birthday card and a little bag of candy. She told me, "You'll be coming to my house for dinner tonight." Mama had an appointment and wasn't able to pick me up after school.

The principal drove me in her black car through a neighborhood where each house was edged with a white picket fence. She unlocked the door and, with a sweeping hand, welcomed me into her home. I tugged down my too small t-shirt and stood in the dark wooden doorway, unsure of what to do.

"Go in," she encouraged.

Her living room was enormous. I froze in the hallway when I heard my footsteps echo on the hardwood floor.

The principal said, "Come in, come in."

She pointed to a chair near the dining table. I climbed up onto it, and it felt like a king's chair. I ran my hands down its sleek arms. She brought me a coloring book and some crayons in a plastic tub.

"Color in this while I go make macaroni and cheese for dinner."

I left the book in front of me unopened and looked quickly around the room. I felt like a robber in the strange room. Behind my chair was a tall, dark shelf filled with leaning books of all different sizes and colors. Did the books know that I didn't belong in this house?

She caught me peeking at them when she came back and smiled. "Those books are old friends."

After dinner, she poured out a plastic bag filled with seashells on top of the table with a clatter, and we glued the flat shells onto paper. In a low, gentle voice, the principal asked me questions about my home life. How often did I eat? Did I get to see my dad? How did I get that bruise? I picked up a white seashell, held it over my eye like a patch, and then spun it in my fingers.

"This seashell lost his brother," I said, pretending not to understand her questions.

I was afraid to talk about Mama. I didn't know why, but our life was a secret, and Mama would be mad at me if I said anything. I rattled off a story about the seashell, hoping to distract her. After gluing it to the yellow construction paper, I ran my fingers through the pile of shells scattered across the table.

"Maybe this is him!" I pointed, frantic not to give her an opportunity to speak again. She looked at me, and then walked into the kitchen to get ice cream. She didn't ask me any more questions.

The principal dropped me off that evening, and she spoke to Mama through the opened car window, "We had a great time! She's had dinner and ice cream."

Inside the apartment Mama frowned at me, "You sure have her fooled. She spoils you rotten. If she knew you, she wouldn't like you."

I ran into my room with my shell art paper. I didn't want to make her even angrier by being on her side of the house. I never told her about how the principal had asked me questions.

A few days later, Mama picked me up from school and we drove to the store. I waited in the car while she went in. She came out carrying two ice-cream cones. I bounced up and down on the seat grinning with surprise. She pinched the two of them in one hand while she wrestled the car door open and then passed one over to me. As I ate it, I wondered if it meant something was different in our relationship. Maybe she wanted to be around me now? I held the vanilla ice cream like it was proof that Mama loved me. As slow as possible I savored each bite, rolling it in my mouth. I didn't want the proof to disappear, but couldn't figure out a way to save the cone without it getting mushy.

We sat in the Pontiac without talking. Mama stared out at some far-off point through the car's windshield. I tried to see what interested her; nothing but a light pole. She turned her ice cream cone upside down and shook it hard twice. I looked over again, was she doing a magic trick?

"Why did you shake your ice-cream cone?" I almost put my hand over my mouth for being so dumb to question her. I was afraid she would use her scary voice.

She gave a little twitch and glanced over at me. In a flat tone, she said, "I don't remember doing that. " We both turned back to look out the window and continued to eat in silence.

When we returned home, I followed her into the dark living room with the shaggy orange carpet. Will Mama let me be in the same room as her? She gave me a look, and I wondered if I had tracked in dog doo on my shoe.

"What are you doing in here? Go play in your room."

On the way back to my room, I thought, what am I still doing wrong? I wanted to fix it so that Mama would think I was a good girl.

On a cold afternoon, a few weeks later, Mama's brother came over. It had snowed all night, and I could hear them talking with excited voices.

Then Mama yelled, "CeeCee! Get in the car!"

I scrambled into my jacket, and the three of us piled into the Pontiac.

Leaning close to the window, I breathed out on to the glass to watch it fog and drew swirls and dots with the thumb of my knitted mitten. The snow on the ground was so beautiful, clean, and white.

The car gave a hard jerk, and my head bobbed. Mama drove off the road, through the crunching icy grass, and then out onto the frozen lake. I recognized the big warning signs with a giant, red "X" through them. The signs meant stay off the ice. I spun around to look out the rear window at the distancing shore line. Did Mama drive out onto the lake by accident? Did she see the big red "X"?

Mama gave a crazy laugh as she revved the Pontiac, and we flew out into the middle of the lake. I caught our reflections in the rear-view mirror; she was grinning from ear to ear and my face was white. Pictures flashed through my mind--- ice breaking and all of us trapped in the car, drowning in the dark water. Mama jerked the wheel, and we snapped into a hard spin, causing me to fly across the vinyl seat. My fingers dug into the slippery seat but I couldn't stop myself. I hit the window hard with my shoulder, crying out in pain. They laughed even harder the faster the car spun around.

When Mama heard me, she said, "Oh Crap! Don't be such a crybaby. Do you want me to give you something to cry about?"

Pinned against the side window I stared out the window at the spinning world. I squeezed my mitten tight over my mouth.

Mama spun the Pontiac in tight circles eight or ten more times, while I hung tight on-to the window handle. On the last spin my uncle said, "Whoa, the ice is a bit thin here." I held my breath, only letting it out when she turned the car back for the shore.

That night and over the next few days the snow fell hard, until it was up to my waist. One night, after it finally slowed, Mama called me to get my jacket on. I raced around my room, looking for my jacket.

"Now CeeCee!" Mama yelled.

I caught a glimpse of the jacket sleeve poking out from under the pile of blankets on my bed. I shrugged it on and ran out to the car.

My uncle was already in the passenger seat, waiting for me to climb in. Mama was drumming her hands against the steering wheel while I climbed into the back seat. She took off into the black night. We raced over a hill and around a bend in the road, where we shot straight into a car accident. Screaming, she swerved and stomped the brakes. The Pontiac slammed against something I didn't see. I flew in the air and into the back of the driver's seat with a slam, crumpling to the floor.

Mama asked whether everyone was ok, and burst into tears. I

pulled myself up. The other car's bright headlights were bright, and there were dark shadows of people outside the car. I looked over to see why Mama was crying--was she hurt?-- and put my hand on her shoulder.

Mama turned to my uncle. He comforted her with a low, soothing voice, "It's fine, everything is ok."

They were silhouetted in the beaming headlights, and I watched Mama's outline hug his. My body ached to be hugged by her, but I pulled my jacket tight around myself and pushed back into the corner of the seat. Neither of them noticed me. Somehow, I had failed again. It must have been when I hit the back of the seat, I screwed up then. I kept failing these tests to prove that I was a good girl.

A few days later Mama said we were going out to eat with my grandparents. I'm not sure if it had to do with the car accident, but now Mama's parents wanted to repair their relationship with Mama. They had disowned her when she married my dad, and were just beginning to talk with her again. She seemed happy that her parents had invited us out to dinner.

The restaurant we went to had a fancy sign rimmed in blinking yellow lights. Mama examined her reflection in the window and brushed her long brown hair back from her face. Her face was tight when she warned me, "You be on your best behavior." She grabbed the back of my arm, pinching me hard as a warning, and guided me to where my grandparents waited.

The waiter came over to the four of us and led us to a round table. Grandma said hi to Mama, but Grandpa only had eyes for me.

He leaned over smiling at me, "CeeCee, my dear, what would you like to order?"

Mama flashed me an intense look from behind her menu, so I tried to order something that wouldn't make her mad. I squirmed, as the grownups watched me. The menu was heavy with a cloth cover, and I turned the pages as fast as I could, smiling when I saw a picture of spaghetti without sauce. When the waiter came to my corner of the table I pointed to it.

"I would like this, please," I said in my most grown up voice.

"Ohhh,"Mama said in a syrupy sweet voice, "You won't like that." Eyes wide, I looked over at her. She frightened me with her nice tone. I turned the pages in the menu as fast as possible while the grown-ups stared at me, and tried to find more pictures. I didn't want to mess up again. The words were sprawled-out long and slanted, and didn't look like the Bob books I read at school.

Grandpa cleared his throat, and said to me, "Well, if that's what you want, then that's what you'll have."

The waiter nodded, "Oh, you'll enjoy it." I shut my menu with a sick feeling, and Mama shot daggers at me from behind her menu.

The spaghetti came buttered and it tasted like crayons. I hated it. Mama laughed, "I knew it! Dad, you wasted food on CeeCee! Eat it all, little girl." She smiled when I gagged on the food, and kicked my leg under the table.

I didn't want to go home after dinner. She'd warned me to behave, and I failed. When we got home, Mama hit me with her wooden paddle, holding me by the back of my shirt. Whack! Whack! Whack!

"You think you're so smart! I'll show you for shaming me. Count these out!" she said.

Tears ran in my mouth and I couldn't keep count with the smacks. "Sixteen, seventeen, eighteen...."

"Count louder! I can't hear you!"

The blows fell harder and faster, and I screamed to her to please stop. She counted out the last few herself, "Twenty-three, twenty-four, twenty-five!"

She didn't talk to me for a few days after that. I had embarrassed her in front of her father. Mama had told me before that he was the best father in the world, and I was to be a good girl around him so that he would see she was a good mom.

He took Grandma and Mama out shopping about a month later, while I stayed at the house with a babysitter. When they returned from the mall, Grandpa said he had a surprise for me. A surprise! Oh boy! I jumped up and down.

"What is it? Let me see!" He held out a new doll.

My grandparents had been fighting in the car the whole way home about this doll, and Grandma was still protesting.

"That's not a doll for a little girl! I told you not to buy it!"

He ignored her and gently put the fancy doll in my hands. She wore a green, velvet dress, and her brown hair was long and sleek, braided with ribbons and silk flowers. Her name was Mary Jane.

In a sugar-sweet voice, Mama said to Grandma, "It's ok, Mom." And then she turned to me, "Look at what Grandpa bought you

CeeCee! Isn't she pretty? You will take good care of her, won't you?"

It was the first doll I owned. She was beautiful. I loved her because Mama looked at me when she said the doll was pretty.

Weeks later, Grandma bought me a huge Kewpie doll. "Now this is the type of doll a little girl would want to play with," she said.

The Kewpie doll was the size of my friend's two-year-old sister. I bit my lip when I saw how my grandparents watched me closely, waiting to see which doll I chose to play with. I didn't want to lose the love of either of them, so I carried both dolls slung under my arms.

Kewpie was heavy and wore real baby clothes and my old brown shoes. I had green play-doh stuck in the bottom of those shoes. One night in my room, I wrapped my arms around her waist and pretended she was hugging me good-night. Her arms were hard though, so I pushed her away from me, disappointed.

Sometimes I brought Kewpie to the Smith's house. They were Mama's friends, and I stayed with them if I wasn't at preschool. They had a three-year-old daughter, Chelsea, and we watched Captain Kangaroo on their black-and-white TV, sitting on a messy sofa that was half-covered with piles of unfolded laundry. One time as Chelsea and I played with our dolls together, she grabbed for my doll's dress when I was changing her, and wouldn't give it back.

I pulled on it, "It's mine! Give it back!"

We had a tug-of-war over the pink baby dress. She wouldn't let go, so I boxed her ears. Her mom ran into the bedroom when Chelsea screamed and rushed to comfort her. I stared, as Holly scooped her daughter up onto her lap. She gently smoothed the hair back off of Chelsea's forehead and kissed her. There was a lump in my throat when Holly wiped her daughter's tears; I didn't know a mother's hands could be so gentle. She cuddled her daughter, and I looked away. A deep hollow echoed inside me.

Holly turned to me defensively. "Do you want your ears boxed?" I shook my head no. She asked, "Do I need to tell your mom?"

"Please don't tell her," I begged. Holly didn't like me anymore and I couldn't fix it, even by saying that I was sorry.

~ 5 ~
THE BROWN HOUSE

When I was four-and-a-half, Mama and I moved out of the city apartment and into a small country town in Pennsylvania. I still didn't see Dad and didn't understand why.

Our new home had brown shingles that covered all the sides. The owner met us there and gave Mama the keys while I ran around the outside and counted out the five windows. The owner was an old woman in a plaid shirt and blue jeans named Mrs. Perkins.

She puffed out her chest and said, "This house has been home to many generations of the Perkins family."

I looked at the brown house. They must have been small to fit so many in there.

Mrs. Perkins lived at the bottom of the hill, down the black top road that twisted past our home. I spent hours running over the hills around the house, because Mama wanted me to stay outside all the time. My hair bleached white from the time in the sun.

A few weeks later someone dropped off two kittens at our house, one all black and one striped gray. The black kitten tried to scamper up the lilac tree, its tiny nails getting stuck in the bark. It tried to free itself with little jerks, and Mama laughed. She pulled its nails out of the tree and held it against her face.

"Such a sweet baby!"

Mama sat in the sunshine on the front stoop, and stroked the kitten.

"Such a pretty girl, such a good girl."

I stood quiet under the lilac and watched hungrily.

She brought the kittens inside, and I escaped to my meadow, scrubbing the tears from my eyes.

The field always made me feel better. I'd run through the tall grass and squeal at the spit bugs that made my tan legs wet. Or, watch a daddy-long-leg as he picked along the ground with thread-like legs. My favorite part was lying back in the grass. It towered around me in waving green walls, giving me a rectangular window of the blue sky.

One day, Mama said to me, "Go on down to your aunt's house. Your cousin's going to meet you."

Our little brown house was a few miles away from Mama's sister and the cousins. Mama often sent me to walk to their house during the years we lived there.

I felt brave walking down the paved road that ran by my house. The hot sun melted the black tar in the asphalt and it stuck to the bottoms of my shoes. My littleness felt magnified every time a car rushed past me as the wind tugged at my clothes and hair. I was scared to walk on the road by myself, afraid I might get lost, but couldn't say that to Mama. My blue sneakers walked the white line like a tightrope with my arms flung out to balance. I am big enough for this wide world. I take care of myself.

After about a mile-and-a-half, I turned left onto a dirt road. Christy was already halfway up the road to meet me. I ran up to give her a hug, and we walked with arms linked together. The maple tree branches touched overhead, making a long autumn tunnel. It was rare for a car to travel down it, and the deep tire ruts were hidden beneath a thick carpet of orange maple leaves. We jumped and crunched through the leaves and swung broken branches through the bushes on the side of the road.

"What was that?" she said, making her eyes big to scare me. She ended up spooked herself, so we sang made-up nursery rhymes at the top of our voices to drown out any creepy forest noises. That night, my aunt packed me in her car and dropped me off at my home. My smile fell off my face as I walked through the front door. Mama was still cuddling her kittens as I hurried to my room.

I had a sick stomach the next day, and preschool wouldn't take me. Mama rushed around the house trying to get ready.

"Walk over to Shelby's house. She's going to watch you today," she said, whipping a brush through her hair.

I nodded and put my blue sneakers on, the laces flapping as I ran out the door.

Shelby was a teenager who lived on the other side of the thick woods that sat on the far side of the hill. The trail to her house was muddy and thin, and wove like a snake through the dark woods. The fallen leaves didn't crunch here. Instead, they lay in brown wet piles at the base of the trees, and the smell made me feel even sicker. I hurried along the trail and tried not to imagine the big bad wolf I had learned about in preschool.

Shelby opened the back door right as I shot out of the woods. She watched me run across her back yard.

She leaned out and yelled, "What's the password? Just kidding, come on in."

We went through the laundry room where I left my sneakers next to a pair of rubber boots. I followed her to her bedroom, and my mouth dropped open. Her room was filled with a rainbow of colors-- shoes, jewelry, and stuffed animals-- and her clothing overflowed out of the dresser. She had a frilly bed with a pink bedspread and bed ruffle that came from the store. I had never seen anything like it.

She caught me staring, and said, "It's called a canopy. I've had it for years." She flicked the lace with her finger. "It's getting too young for me now."

She handed me a plastic bag off of the bed. "Here's some stuff I've outgrown, just a couple things."

I peeked in the bag. Among the clothing was a black-and-white dog lamp. I giggled when I saw it, never thinking I could own such a prize.

Just then, my stomach gave a squeeze of nausea, so Shelby told me to go lie on the couch. I nibbled on saltines all day and stared at an ugly painting of a black vase filled with flowers that hung on the wall.

That night, when I got home, I tore through the bag to look for the dog-lamp. But it wasn't there-- a large hole was. Somehow, I had lost my treasure on the trail when I hurried home in dread of the shadow monsters. I sunk to my bed and started to cry.

When Mama picked me up from preschool the next day, my aunt was in the car next to her, and bags of groceries were in the back seat. At our house, I scrambled out of the car after my aunt through the passenger door. She didn't see me and slammed the heavy door shut on my finger.

Pain exploded to my elbow. I didn't make a sound, instead gasped and tried to pull myself free. My aunt turned around and yelled, "Hurry up! What the heck is your problem?" Her eyebrows flew up when she saw my finger pinched white in the door. I cried as she wrenched the car door open, and my finger throbbed. Mama walked away into the house. My aunt examined my finger and hustled me into the kitchen. I whimpered when she held my hand under the cold water.

A week later my nail dangled and was an awful shade of purple. Chelsey's dad examined it when we went over for dinner.

"Would you like me to pull it off?"

I nodded, and he took me into a dark room.

"This will just take a second, don't cry."

He ripped it off. It came off so quick I didn't have time to wince. I put the nail in my pocket, and that night, taped it to my cardboard kitchen oven at home.

Several weeks later, Preschool was closed for a holiday. Early the next morning Mama got me up before the sun was up.

"Hurry and get ready. You're coming to work with me."

She did the billing at the local auto parts shop. When we walked into the big, dirty building, the bright fluorescent lights hurt my eyes. I had to trot to keep up with her, but was too excited to care. The bland room was a let-down, with only an old desk and wall of gray filing cabinets.

She gestured to the desk, "Climb under there."

I looked at the small space with my fists over my mouth. She snapped her fingers in impatience. I crawled under the desk, quickly turning around to look out.

She bent down and said, "Don't make a sound, or I'll get fired."

Her hand appeared several minutes later holding a pencil and a small square of paper. I smiled at her gift. I'm going to make her a pretty picture!

She scooted her chair in and blocked the bright office light. I blinked my eyes to adjust to the dark. Mama wore a skirt, and when she turned to answer the phone, her bare legs moved from one side to the other, brushing against me.

She didn't like that and whispered in an angry tone, "Don't touch them!"

I curled my body up a little more into the corner while I used the back of the desk to draw on.

Hours later, my pretty picture had collapsed into a messy, dark drawing because every inch of the paper had been colored on. I was hungry, and cramped, and had to go to the bathroom. I squirmed, hoping the coast would be clear soon, so that we could go home.

One Saturday soon after that day, she rushed around the house to get dressed. She put on a cute skirt and her favorite strappy sandals. There were beads on the toes like little candies.

"Let's go," she said, and I climbed into the back. We drove for a long time. The sun heated the vinyl so I scooted to the other side of the seat.

Mama pulled into a driveway and we got out. Before Mama knocked on the door, she smoothed down her long hair and put a bright smile on her face. It was rare when I saw her smile, and I loved to see it appear, like a magic trick. She didn't knock on the door, but walked right in. Everyone greeted her with loud cheers. I walked behind her with a big smile, like I was with a famous person. She flicked her finger towards the kitchen and told me to wait there for her and stay quiet.

I sat on a kitchen stool waiting for Mama to finish her visit and looked around. The window by the sink was filled with stained glass animals, and seashells. My stomach growled, and I giggled, poking at it, trying to make it growl more. When that no longer worked I leaned back to look through the doorway into the living room to see what the grownups were doing. My room was quiet and dark, and their room was loud with laughter and men's voices. I watched for a few minutes, they kept laughing but I didn't understand what was so funny. Grown-ups are weird.

A man walked into the kitchen and grabbed a bag of chips. I sat up quick, heat flooded my cheeks at being caught looking into the grownup room. He came over to me.

"Hey kiddo, you want something to eat? Want some chips?"

Was Mama watching? I snatched the food and shoved it into my mouth with a mumbled thank you.

Mama looked around the corner, and caught me chewing. She spanked me that night.

"What did I say about bothering my friends?"

I screamed I was sorry, and couldn't sit down when she finished.

She took me with her to another party a few weeks later. I rested my head on the table, tired. My legs hurt from dangling, and I drummed them against the chair. Mama and another lady came in to get a beer, so I sat up. Mama's friend brought over a glass of ice water and a carrot for me. I looked at Mama, and she nodded. I took a big bite out of the carrot, and crunched it fast, and then took a gulp of the water, and inhaled an ice cube. Choking, I hopped off my chair. Mama popped the cap off a beer, and handed the opener to her friend. I clawed at my throat, and tried to gasp that I couldn't breathe. Mama stared at me with owl eyes, but she didn't move. Her friend came over and rubbed my back to soothe me.

"You're ok honey, it will go down, don't worry."

The friend hurried to the sink and ran the hot water until it was steaming. She filled a glass for me to drink. "Drink this, it will push it down."

I tried to drink it while she continued to rub and pat my back. The ice cube slid down, and I burst into tears. I looked around the kitchen for Mama, but she wasn't there. The friend patted my back for another second.

"You're all right," Mama's friend said, before disappearing through the kitchen door.

I walked back to my stool and sat, and bit my thumb nail. Was I was in trouble for bothering Mama's friend? I didn't want to be hit with the paddle. When we got home that night I got into bed still dressed, pulled the covers to my neck and pretended I was asleep while I listened for her.

We went to the same house again for another party the next weekend. A man brought me into the dark living room. Mama's friends sat on couches and chairs in a semi-circle. "You stand here," he said, "Hold this." He handed me a smoking stub held in a metal clip.

The red coal on the tip was hot. "I don't want to get burned." I looked for someone to hand it to.

"It's fine. Quit whining," Mama said from her spot on the couch.

I brought it to each of them whenever they gestured to me. They put it in their mouths like a cigarette, and there was lots of smoke and laughter. The smoke smelled terrible, but I liked the feathers tied with leather that dangled from the end of the clip. I marched up and saluted the man when he waggled his fingers towards me, and he winked and saluted me back.

Mama rolled her head along the man's shoulder she was sitting next to, waving at me with a floppy hand. She looked at the glowing stub and snatched it from me without touching my fingers. After a big drag she handed it back, dropping it a split second before I had a hold of it. I grabbed at the leather thong, and the red coal swung up to my wrist. I squealed, and nearly threw it, but the man plucked it from my fingers. He laughed like I had done something funny, and soon everyone in the room was laughing. My important feeling wilted, and the hollowness in me boomed.

~ 6 ~
TONSILS

Winter came, and the whole world that had once looked like it had been put to bed under a giant patchwork quilt, was now brown with rotten leaves. Along with the cold temperatures came a horrible virus. I was not quite five, and never been sicker. Air felt stale and used up, and I went outside to feel the breeze on my face, hoping it would help me breathe.

I was sick for several months before Mama took me to the doctor. The doctor peered at my throat with his bright light. He told Mama that my tonsils were infected and had banded together with scar tissue. When we got home that day, I ran to the bathroom and said "AHHHHH," with my face inches from the mirror. I wanted to see what a tonsil was.

Soon after that doctor's appointment, Mama came over to where I sat in the kitchen eating cereal. She stared at my mouth. I paused with my spoon in the air.

"You need to breathe quieter, right now."

I took a few wheezy breaths. She backhanded me across my face.

"Quit defying me."

Tears blurred my vision, and I put my head down on the table.

"You look like a donkey with your mouth open! Heee Haw Heee Haw."

I didn't move until Mama walked away.

That night, she heard me in my bed and yelled, "Quiet down now!"

I hugged my pillow over my face and listened for her footsteps. I chanted into my pillow, "Can't breathe yet, don't breathe." There were little sparkles in the dark, and my chest pounded. She didn't come in.

The next afternoon, my uncle came to our house with a pizza. He threw it on the counter and then jumped over the back of the couch with a thump to watch TV. Mama sat next to him, and they flipped through the channels; laughing game shows, droning news channels, before they settled on a movie with scary music. I stayed in the kitchen at the table with my plate.

Without turning around from the TV, Mama yelled, "Stop! Your breathing is ruining our show. We can't even hear what they are saying!"

Mama and my uncle looked at each other then and mimicked me with bulging eyes, and open mouths to let out loud gasps. Both of them laughed and Mama gave a couple of donkey brays. I stared at the pizza in my hands. My face felt hot, and the hollowness echoed in my heart.

It was late spring when Mama scheduled the surgery for my tonsils. The sky was blue and clear when she drove me to the hospital. We sat in silence in the hospital room on either side of a bright square of sunshine on the floor. She was frozen like a statue, hands resting on the seat of her metal chair, blank eyes staring at the mossy green hospital room wall. I didn't make a sound, my legs dangling. I slowly swung my leg, making my untied shoelace spin in circles.

The doctor apologized when he walked in. His face was red, and he talked fast.

"Sorry, sorry. Busy day. Let's see what we got."

The doctor pushed my tongue down with a wooden stick, and I wanted to gag. He peered through a silver mirror, and I could see my face in it, upside down. I tipped my head to see if I could make my face pop up-right. He flipped the silver dish up with a snap and gave a disappointed sigh. Squeaking back in the chair, he turned to Mama.

"We can't do the surgery. Your daughter is sick again. Too dangerous. Let's reschedule for two weeks and see how she's doing then." He patted me on the head, stood up, and walked out of the room with large steps.

Mama was very angry, and she glared out the windshield on the way home.

"If you could have been a big girl, and kept your fingers out of your mouth you wouldn't be sick. I'll make sure your fingers are out of your mouth."

She slapped my face many times over the next few days. I held the bottom of my shirt every time I was near her, stretching it down to keep my hands far from my face, and flinched when I saw her move hers.

Two weeks later, as I climbed into the car to return to the hospital, Mama twisted back in the front seat. Her face creased with dark lines around her eyes and mouth.

"You better not be sick again."

We waited at the hospital the same way as before. When the doctor came in to check me, I was shaking. Please say yes, please say yes.

"Now, no reason to be scared," the doctor said, and he smiled and winked at me. When he was done examining my throat, he tapped my shoulder. "Okay, looks good. Let's get this taken care of!"

It was my fifth birthday. I pulled out a doll that wore yellow pajamas from my coat pocket that Grandma had given me the day before.

"Behave," Mama said, and walked out of the room.

A nurse came in and gave me funny pajamas. They had blue stars on them and lots of ribbon. She spun me around and tied the ribbons down my back. "You just wait here a sec. I'm sending in our special nurse to help you feel better."

I swung my legs in the chair for a little bit, waiting for the next nurse. She walked in pushing a wheel chair.

"Hop in. We're going for a ride."

"Where are we going?" I asked.

"You need to be a big girl now," she said with a small smile.

The hallway was dark, with two doors sat at the end like a giant insect mouth. Adults walked around in blue gowns, and some wore white masks. Their eyes were dark and shiny. Why are they covering their faces? What are they hiding?

She pushed open the doors, and there was noise and bright lights. Patting the bed, she told me to climb up. I shook my head no, so she boosted me with her arms tight around my waist. "Lie down. I don't want you to fall."

A man was suddenly at my other side, his hand on my wrist. My heart beat faster, and I jerked away.

"Let me go!"

He leaned in. Even his eyes were covered with glasses. "Do you know how to count backwards?"

I looked at him and started to cry. I didn't want to cooperate anymore. More nurses crowded around me and pinned me down. I kicked at them. The male nurse held the mask over my face with firm hands. My tears ran down into my ears.

"Count down from one hundred please." My vision doubled, and then I was out.

I saw witches. The doctors had long warty noses and evil black eyes. They came at my mouth with sharp knives, and I couldn't move no matter how hard I tried. When I woke up, I was crying again. A nurse popped her head from behind an orange curtain. I held my throat; searing pain. "Would you like some ice-cream? You have to stop crying if you want some."

I nodded and closed my eyes.

I woke up again in another room. There was a screech, and a little kid next to me jumped up and down in a covered crib. He looked at me and made a face. A few minutes passed, while he hooted and bounced until another nurse with a mask wheeled him out.

Mama picked me up the next day. I left my doll behind in my hospital bed when Mama led me from the room. I didn't understand we were leaving the hospital.

Mama said, "I'm not going to turn around to get it. It serves you right. You don't take care of your toys." Her steps were quick and echoed in the parking garage, and I hurried to keep up with her. Tears burned my eyes; having my breathing fixed was not going to make her happy with me. Still not making eye contact she said, "By the way, this surgery was your birthday present."

The next day I stayed home alone with a cup of cold water to sip. Mama had to work.

When she came home that night she sent me down to the mailbox. There was a brown package there for me from Grandma on Mama's side. Grandma gave me a bible for my birthday, with red letters for when Jesus spoke, and a middle section full of bright colored pictures. I held it in my hands, grinning at its heavy richness.

"You take care of that, CeeCee. It cost Grandma a lot of money."

I nodded and tucked it under my arm to my room. Pushing my clothes to the floor, I sat on the bed and flipped the pages to the colorful pictures. I stopped when I came to a picture of Jesus holding little children on his lap, and fell in love. Tracing over the little children with my finger, I tried to decide which one I was. Was I the blonde one who had Jesus' hand on her head? Or could I be the one with the brown curls he looked at with kind eyes? I ran my hands over my hair and felt how short, thin and unkempt it was. I was neither of those pretty girls. I shoved the bible under my bed.

A few nights later I walked down the tarry road to Mrs. Perkins' house. Mama was going on a date. Mrs. Perkins made me chocolate pudding while I waited on the couch with the funny tassels along the edge. She put a spoonful of cool whip on it and brought the dish to me as we settled in to watch The Waltons. When the show was over she went to the corner and pulled out a metal stool. Dragging it to the book shelf she lifted a big, egg-shaped doll.

"This is a Russian nesting doll." Her gray hair bobbed as she climbed down from the stool and set it on the table. She pulled the first two pieces apart, showing me the next bright painted face. I clapped. She pushed it over. "Here, you try."

I opened the next doll, and carefully matched the two pieces together. I laughed when I got to the baby. So darling. Mrs. Perkins's glossy dining room table became a little cottage house for the wooden dolls.

Mrs. Perkins didn't understand Mama's strict rules with me. Mrs. Perkins liked to talk with me, and we went on walks together while my gray cat followed us. She taught me how to pick butter cups and hold them to my skin to see if I liked butter. She told me a story about forget-me-nots--the tiny flowers that were afraid to be forgotten-- and I giggled when I saw some.

"I found you!" I ran up to point them out to Mrs. Perkins, and my cat followed. He curled up around my legs and rubbed his cheek against the tiny flowers.

Mama had warned her before we left, "You want to walk with her? That girl'll talk your ear off. Don't let her take advantage of you."

Mrs. Perkins answered her, "Oh, she's delightful to walk with!" Mama laughed, but Mrs. Perkins insisted, "She's fine." Mama gave a quick nod.

Mama told me in private, "Mrs. Perkins doesn't know you very well, CeeCee. You sure have her fooled." I was scared. I didn't know how to keep the fact that I was a monster hidden from Mrs. Perkins, so that she would continue to like me.

A few weeks after my birthday a classmate knocked into me when we all rushed to go play on the swing-set outside. The back of my head smacked against the glass door. Reaching back, I examined the lump, and my hand came away bloody. I looked at my bloody hand in shock. How am I going to hide this? I didn't want to tell anyone.

The teacher walked behind me.

"Oh my!" she said, when she saw the blood. She disappeared for a minute, and returned with a wad of paper towels.

"Hold this tight, and let's go see the nurse." She called to the other teacher, "Watch my kids, I'll be back in a minute."

My teacher walked me to the school nurse while I held the towels to my head. The nurse peeled back the towels for a minute and quickly turned to the phone.

"Please don't call my mom! I'm okay, honest I am." I pleaded.

Her eyes flickered over at me and she smiled, before she was distracted again. "Oh, hello? Yes, I'm calling about your daughter. She's had a bit of an accident and it might be good to see a doctor." I crumpled down on the cot, shivering. I was going be in big trouble.

Thirty minutes passed, until a man walked in the office. He looked like a stranger, until his features melted into a face I knew. Dad was here. I was so relieved that he was the one who came, that I didn't feel shy.

Parked in front of the school entrance was Dad's new red convertible. It was so fancy. Dad must be a rich man. He drove fast, while I held the paper towels on my head, trying to keep the ice from slipping.

"Where are we going?"

He didn't answer. Instead, he fumbled with his silver zippo trying to light his cigarette. It fell in his lap, and he said a bad word.

He parked his car in front of the hospital.

"Don't slam the door!" he said, when I got out. He walked with me into the building with his eye already on a plastic chair. As he sat down, a nurse came over to us. Dad waved, "Go on."

The nurse steered me by my shoulder into a big room. It was dark, with a single bed covered by a paper sheet under a light. She picked me up and set me on the bed, hurting my armpits when she lifted me. The doctor came out of the dark without a sound, and I jumped. He swiveled the bright light over behind me and poked my head.

"We need to cut the hair."

My hair? "No! No! No! Leave me alone!" I screamed, pushing against the paper to jump off. Firm hands grabbed me.

"You stay here. You want your head to get better, don't you?" The nurse held my wrist and forearm, and her hands squeezed tight.

I heard them ask for a needle and cat gut. "I want a Band-Aid! Don't put cat guts in my hair!" No one answered me. The doctor and nurses faces looked angry before they held me down on the table and stitched my scalp. They worked in silence. I screamed.

As we left the hospital, Dad told me not to get blood on the leather of his new car. I sniffled in the seat next to him. He dropped me back off at the school and drove away as soon as I shut the car door. I walked into the school and stood there in the empty hallway, the back of my head shaved and cold. With a lump in my throat, the hollowness echoed inside of me.

Mama was mad when I got home from school that night. She didn't like the stitches, and she didn't like that Dad had a new car. She made goulash for dinner, out of noodles and cans of white potatoes and tomatoes. I hated goulash.

"Don't turn your nose up at it, we're poor. Your Dad doesn't love you enough to help take care of you, but he sure has enough money to buy that fancy new car."

Saturday night Mama had a date, and I was going along. It was dark when we left for a diner. We sat at a long counter on tall stools, and she fidgeted with the paper napkin in front of her, folding and refolding it. I tried to fold mine, but no interesting shapes came out of it, so I tore it into a little nest instead. Her date didn't show up. I didn't like the grilled cheese I had ordered, because it tasted like the plastic was still on the cheese. When we got home she spanked me with the wooden paddle of a paddle ball toy.

"You don't embarrass me when I tell you to eat. If I tell you to jump you say how high!" Mama spanked me until I screamed, and kept up until she broke the paddle on me.

Mama bought another paddle ball the next time we went to the grocery store. The clerk smiled at me.

"Getting a prize?"

Mama shook her head, "Niece's birthday present."

I turned away, my attention caught by my first wiggly tooth. I sucked at it, and then pressed my tongue hard against it and tasted blood. Mama frowned when she saw me wiggling the tooth. "Pull it out!"

The checker over heard her. "I bet your little girl would pull her tooth out if she could have this little bag of peanuts! Wouldn't you like these peanuts sweetheart?"

"Of course," Mama said, and turned to me, opening her eyes wide. "Pull it out, and you can have them." She dangled the bag of peanuts out of my reach. I was hungry.

I tried to pull it, but it was still too firmly fastened in my gum. I lifted my hand a few inches in the striped bag's direction. "Please Mama." My mouth was watering.

She jerked them away. "You pull it." She smiled and fear zipped through me.

The checker's mouth opened into an "O" at Mama's response, and she said to me, "Here honey, just take the peanuts. My treat."

Mama frowned at her. "If she can't pull the tooth, then she doesn't deserve peanuts."

I couldn't do it, and missed out on the treat. When we got home, Mama cut the ball off of the paddle and threw it in the trash.

"Now, just you try and smart off."

When I finally lost my tooth a week later, Mama told me to put it under my pillow. "The tooth fairy will come," she said.

The light in the room was gray the next morning when I woke up. Mama slapped the wall above my head again.

"Get up! You're late!"

I jumped out of bed and pulled on the clothes I had worn the day before. Grabbing my lunch bag, I ran out the door, making it to the bus stop just as the orange bus turned the corner at the bottom of the hill belching black smoke.

It was until after dinner that I remembered. The tooth fairy! I ran into my room and flipped back the pillow. My tooth was gone. A quarter was there inside a twisted cellophane cigarette wrapper. A fairy came into my room last night! She left me a prize! I ran out to show Mama.

"CeeCee, nice things would happen to you all the time if you'd just be a good girl."

"Mama, I will try to be better! I'll turn over a new leaf! I love you!" I said, holding my hand over my heart.

Mama said she didn't believe me. "You'd do what I want if you really loved me."

I walked away from her with my head hanging back to my room. It was dark in the room, with the moon light shining on the lilac bush outside my window.

I flipped on the light and climbed the bed to study the window, looking for tiny pin-holes where a fairy might have climbed inside. How did the tooth fairy get in here? My reflection looked back at me, her hand touching mine through the glass. I began to jump up and down on my bed, and stare at her. She looked like a little girl, with blonde flyaway hair and skinny, bug bitten legs. I felt so much older than her. Who are you? *bounce* Are you actually me? Do you walk the roads alone? *Bounce* Do you vacuum and take care of the chickens like I do? *Bounce*

Also reflected in the window behind her was a cartoon poster that hung over my bed. The poster was of an old woman with a hefty wooden spoon and a scowl, dirty children hanging out of a giant shoe. Mama had once told me that I was like one of the woman's bratty kids. Which one am I? I rubbed my thumb over the blonde girl hiding behind the shoe. Here I am.

Tired from jumping, I flipped off the light and lay in bed with my tongue stuck in the empty slot in my teeth. My bedroom was divided by a piece of white plaster board. Mama slept on her side, and I slept on the other. Her lamp was always on, and the light shone into my dark side through the crack where the board didn't quite meet the wall. The blankets on the bed were a mess. I kicked my legs under them to straighten them and pulled them up under my chin.

Turning, I studied the crack. Can I fit them? I slid my fingers through the space and watched them go from dark to light. My fingers were marching ants as I moved them up and down the wall. There was a soft touch, Mama's fingers against mine. I yanked my fingers back as a thrill shot through me. Rolling closer, my cheek against the cool wall, I looked through the crack, but couldn't see her. I listened, and didn't hear her breathing.

I slid my fingers through again and again; wiggling and making them dance, hoping to get her to touch them again. In a sharp voice she told me to stop. There was scraping as she moved her bed into the living room, taking the lamp with her.

~ 7 ~
THE SECRET

Another summer was trickling away. I would be starting kindergarten soon. My hair was white again from the sun, and I could whistle through the gap of my two missing bottom teeth. The sun stretched through the open front door across my lap, making a shadow-me on floor. I ate a sandwich at the table, chewing and watching a green inch worm slide down its silk thread in the door frame. I stopped, the sandwich half-way to my mouth. Mama hadn't gotten up from her bed in the living room all day. Was she still sleeping?

Setting the sandwich down, I took quiet steps through the kitchen. The living room was dark, and she didn't move on the bed. My heart beat faster as I stepped towards her. The blanket twitched suddenly, when she waved a fly away. I ran outside, snatching my sandwich up on the way out.

The day was extra quiet. When it was dinner-time I went back inside, and pulled out the peanut butter and orange marmalade (yuck, why does Mama get this?) and made myself another sandwich. Still no noise. I wiped the table with my napkin and crumpled it around the crumbs before tossing it in the trash, and went to bed.

I was almost asleep when I heard her moan. My eyes pop opened, seeing funny twirls and blobs as my eyes strained in the dark. What's the matter with Mama? Why is she crying?

The next morning she shuffled to the bathroom with her arms crossed holding her tummy, her face creased with pain wrinkles. She looked over at me standing in the kitchen.

"Don't you tell anyone that your Mama is sick! It's a secret! Don't you tell no-one. Ever!"

She climbed back into her bed afterwards, her body moving in slow starts and pauses, until she finally lay flat with a sigh. From the kitchen I watched her roll to her side and moan from the pain.

"Mama, do you want some water?"

"Leave me be," she groaned, "It's your father who did this to me. We were fine together until I got pregnant with you, then he turned into a crazy person."

I backed away, as tears stung my eyes. I would have done anything to make her better. I didn't know how to fix her except to not be born.

Mama stayed in bed from then on. She had just enough strength to drag herself to the car and drive to the medical clinic week after week for tests. Each time, she came home frustrated. They couldn't figure out what caused her to hurt so much.

It went on for months. She lay hardly moving, groaning with pain on her teeny bed. Before I left for school I put a glass of water by her bed. After I got home from kindergarten I helped her to the bathroom, supporting her as best as I could with her arm around my shoulder. The months whittled her weight down to sixty-seven pounds. She felt like a bundle of sticks in my arms.

I washed her hair while she leaned moaning over the edge of the white bath tub. As gentle as possible, I rubbed in the soap bubbles and then poured water from a cup to rinse it clean.

"Is it rinsed CeeCee? I can't take any more," Mama whimpered.

"I'm done, Mama. I'm done." I patted her hair dry, wrapping it in a towel like a turban on her head, and then she leaned on me on her way back to the bed.

I helped dress her in her loose flannel jammies. She could barely lift her leg, while I slid the bottoms up. I scooted them up to her waist in tiny movements every time she whispered, "Ready."

When her hair dried I brushed it with careful strokes; in the way I always wished she would brush mine. She waved me away with her bony hands, exhausted. I whispered, "Mama, you are beautiful." And she looked at me with her sunken, brown eyes for a moment, before looking away.

After long months, Mama had a diagnosis from the doctor, a

foreign word called _____, and the doctor prescribed Mama some medicine. I found the orange pill bottles lined up on the counter, ready to give to her when she asked. I wrestled to remove the lids and then counted out the weird shaped, colored pills for Mama. Rolling the pills around in my hand, I wondered what they tasted like. Are they sweet? They looked like candy.

One night, Mama was shaking non-stop in her bed. I climbed in the bed with her, biting my nail for a moment before I laid my hand on her shoulder. When she accepted my touch, I held her while she shivered with her knees pulled to her chest. Maybe I can keep her warm, so she won't shake any more. It wasn't often Mama let me do this, and I rested my cheek against her back and closed my eyes, my heart squeezing to feel her so close to me.

The next day, after Mama was settled in her bed, I ran outside to take care of our chickens. The chickens were our prized possessions because the eggs were all the food we had to eat. Mama couldn't work or go to the store. I pulled white socks over my hands and stuck my head into the dark coop to look down the long line of their nesting boxes. The chickens squawked crossly and fluffed their feathers, and bits of straw and tiny feathers floated in the air while I crawled toward the first nest.

"Nice Chicken, good chicken," I wheedled, my hand feeling for the warm egg. Her sharp beak stabbed the back of my hand. I shrank back and tried not to cry. Mama had warned me not to disturb the chickens or they wouldn't lay eggs. I was afraid Mama would hear them squawking from the house, and I would get into trouble.

The queen bee of the roost, a fat old white hen named Tulips, waited at the end. Tulips had two white feathers that waved on stalks at the top of her head, and her squawks were more indignant and louder than the rest. She refused to give up her eggs and used her mean beak when I tried to get under her fat body. I had to leave them.

I opened the chicken door to their yard so they could scratch at the bugs, and ran my basket of eggs into the house. Then, I went back to their yard and grabbed the water pan, muddy now with bits of grass floating across the surface, and carried it over to the water pump underneath the lilac tree. The water pump had a broken seal and didn't work very well. I pumped and pumped the handle. It was heavy and awkward, and each time I pulled the handle down it was harder to pull. I grunted, and pulled it again, nothing but squeaks from the metal grinding together. Finally, there was a splash of water into the pan waiting below-- pump and splash, pump and splash. I wiped my face and dried my hands against my shirt and then heaved the metal pan up against my bony hip. I trundled it through the yard towards the coop.

Mama became sicker. It was rare we spoke, but now, because of the pain, she couldn't tolerate any noise. She still needed me nearby to help her, so I sat all day at a little desk in the living room and colored in my book.

Her weakness meant the house became a mess, even though I tried my best to keep up with the chores. It also meant she didn't have the strength to hit me anymore. I brought her glasses of water, and cooked her plates of yellow scrambled eggs. I put clean sheets on her bed. When she said thank you, I melted and gave her a smile. I couldn't make a noise, but my five year old heart hummed with satisfaction.

My aunt picked me up one day after school. "You're coming home with me. Your Mama had to go in for surgery," she said. I got into the car, and it felt empty without my cousins. Why can't I go home? I know how to take care of myself.

Mama almost died during her emergency surgery. She said when she woke up she felt the hand of God on her shoulder. I was never worried about her dying, so I was surprised to hear her story; I always knew that she would be okay. I took good care of her.

My aunt was grumpy with me while I stayed at her house. She scared me with her gruff commands and rolled her eyes when I didn't understand what she wanted. I knew she didn't like me. I had overheard Mama complaining about me to my aunt before.

When my aunt was at work, my cousins and I had fun. We watched Happy Days together on their tiny TV that ran off a car battery, and made weird sandwiches out of pickles, mayonnaise, mustard, peanut butter and potato chips. My Uncle Henry saw the sloppy messes after we finished, and he made us eat them to teach us not to waste food. The gooey sandwiches tasted gross, but we told each other the color our faces turned while we ate them. Purple! Yours is green! Yours has Polka Dots!

My cousins and I made armpit noises when we were supposed to be asleep, and pushed each other high on the rope swing. My cousin

Christy taught me a hand game-- here is the church, here is the steeple, open the doors, and see all the people. I giggled when I turned my hands over and saw my finger people. I learned how to make a cat's cradle out of looped string, and carried pink yarn twisted around my wrist for a quick game.

One morning I woke up covered in grossness. I had diarrhea in the middle of the night. I sat crying in my bed until my aunt came up the stairs. She was furious. She grabbed me by the shoulders, threw me into a tub of cold water, and told me I was a disgusting child. My cousins were in the bathroom getting ready for school, and I was naked in the tub, my face hot, holding a wet washcloth to my chest. Poop floated in the water, and she dunked me under to wash my hair. That evening I was sent to my Grandparents.

My mind reeled from the quick way my aunt had pulled me from her house because I had been a bad girl. I didn't get a chance to say goodbye to my cousins. I was going to be good for my grandparents, and not get into any more trouble.

They were Mama's parents, and lived in a mobile home in a park. The windows were never opened in their house, and my nose wrinkled at the smell of old perfume. The first day I was there Grandma took a long nap. I sat on the cot in the spare room and played with a tiny monkey she gave me, waiting for Grandma to wake up.

Grandpa came home from work, slamming the front door. I jumped off the cot and ran out to the living room.

"Hi Grandpa!"

"Hi yourself. What for dinner?"

"I don't know?" I sat on the couch, twirling my monkey by its arms.

"What? You didn't make me pot roast and mashed potatoes?" He hung his hat on the hook and smiled at me.

I laughed, and Grandma came down the hall. She fluffed the back of her hair with her fingers. "Come on chickadee. Help me make dinner." I jumped off the couch and ran to the kitchen.

"Let me see you walk as quiet as a butterfly." Grandma said. We washed our hands- Grandma called them patties- and then grabbed the vegetables out of the fridge. Grandma taught me a song.

"Oh mares eat oats and does eat oats and little lambs eat ivy. A kid'll eat ivy too, wouldn't you?"

The song twisted my tongue, and only made sense if I sang it slow. Grandma and I sang it fast while we washed the carrots and celery. It sounded like we had our own special language.

The next day my grandparents went to visit Mama in the hospital, and I was left to stay with a male babysitter. I played on the couch with my toy monkey. After a few minutes, I heard him come out of the bedroom. He stopped in the shadow of the doorway to the living room, his face silhouetted in the gloom staring at me. He didn't say anything. He stared at me like he was hungry. The clock ticked loudly, and his eyes were unblinking. A ball grew in my stomach. I glanced away and didn't dare look up at him again. Dread curled through all my limbs. I couldn't pretend to play with my monkey any longer. I rested my hands on the top of the toy in my lap with my head down.

"CeeCee," he said, "come here…. Want to play a game?" My stomach rolled, something wasn't right. There was no one to keep me safe.

He grabbed my arm and pulled me to the bedroom. He shut the door. I tried to open it, and he leaned his shoulder against it, locking it with a click, and laughed at me.

"Don't be a baby, this is a fun game! I'm not going to hurt you." He told me to kiss --.

I objected, "No! Gross! I don't want to do it."

"Come on, just do it. It will be fun. I have a tootsie roll you can have if you do it. It will be fine, it's just a silly thing. I'll tell your mom you were a good girl here. That will make her happy. Won't that make her happy?"

His pressure became greater and greater and finally I did it.

"That wasn't so bad, was it?" He said, before getting up and leaving the room.

I was ashamed I did such a dirty thing, that I ran to the bathroom and scrubbed my lips raw with a scratchy towel trying to make them clean again. When I opened the bathroom door, he was there waiting, tall and scary. He loomed over me, and wouldn't let me out.

"You better not tell anyone about our little game. If you tell anyone, I'll tell your Mama what a nasty little brat you were while you were here. I will find you and I will hurt you. Zip your lips."

He strode away. I ran to my room and shut the door. Shaking, I sat down and leaned against it.

The clock struck seven, disguising the key in the front door of my grandparents returning. I heard their voices in the living room, and tears blurred my eyes at their normal sound. My legs cramped when I stood up, so I shook them and walked out. I felt like a different person now. I was sure they could tell what happened.

Grandma called to me from the kitchen.

"Did you have a nice time?"

My head felt heavy when I nodded.

"What? I can't hear you."

"Yes Grandma." I picked my monkey up off the couch and cuddled him to my chest, and then walked back to my cot. My stomach hurt. Will Grandma and Grandpa leave me again? But they didn't, and Mama came home a few days later.

I watched Mama closely the first few days she was home from the hospital. She smiled a lot, even when she was alone. I didn't know where my place was any more. Was it at the little table, or was it outside? I hope Mama remembers that I love her.

Mama spoke of the day she was taken to the hospital in whispered reverence. She told me how her father had picked her and drove her to the emergency room. She sighed with happiness as she told me how he had tears in his eyes when he carried her into the hospital.

"He's my knight in shining armor."

"That's good, Mama," I said.

She poured herself some ice tea. I went outside to the fence and sat on the top rail, the tall daisies and blue bells tickling my bare feet that hung down. I heard a swish, and thought it was the cat, but it was Mama.

"Boo!" she said, and I grabbed the fence to keep my balance, so surprised to see her. "Isn't it a beautiful day?" she said, and I nodded, a smile spreading across my cheeks.

Mama picked a few of the daisies and threw the flowers into the air. I laughed to see her act silly, and she laughed too. I wanted to keep her there, laughing with me, and started prattling on about school. Her smile shrank as she stared out at the field. Quick! Think of something funny! She raised her hand, cutting me off.

"Let's just be quiet and listen to the birds sing." So, I looked out at the field, and Mama leaned against the fence. I saw a little robin hopping on the road, and started to tell her, until I remembered to be quiet. It was wonderful, but at the same time, I squirmed inside. If

Mama knew the secret, she wouldn't want me anymore.

The next day I came home from school crying after being teased by a classmate. I lingered next to Mama instead of going straight to my room. She froze for a moment, as though she didn't know what to do, and then pulled me stiffly on to her lap. She let me sit there for a minute. She had never done that before. Mama asked me about one of my fallen tears.

"What's that on my shoulder, a rain drop?"

I was so overwhelmed by her physical touch that I giggled, and rested my head on her thin shoulder. I didn't want to ever climb off her lap; I wanted her to hold me forever. This was the second time I remember Mama touching me when it didn't hurt. I brought those two memories out every night and wrapped them around me like a blanket of Mama's love, before I fell asleep.

~ 8 ~
THE BOYFRIENDS

Mama regained her health and her weight over the next few weeks. Her cheeks grew pinker and she was able to get about the house without help. I even caught her doing a little sashay around the cat, dipping down to scratch the top of her head. I wondered what life would look like now.

I felt sick when I saw every bit of healthy ground she regained was a step away from me. The silent treatment began again. Her dark eyes never met mine unless I was in trouble. I tried to bring her back, by doing the things I had done when she was sick. When I offered to cook eggs, she shook her head.

"No, I don't want that."

I brought her a bouquet of dandelions, and she placed them in a glass with some water, and never looked at them again. When they closed into wilted green pods I threw them out.

Her hands went back to being scary sources of pain. I watched for them to move, and ducked to the side if they came flying at me. She grabbed the back of my arms and pinched with a twist to get my attention. She decided the toy paddles were too wimpy, and used her thick wooden spoons.

"Don't you move, CeeCee, or I will start this all over again." She didn't stop until she was satisfied with my screams and pleas. "That's how I can tell you are genuinely sorry," she said when she put the spoon away.

We drove to the grocery store a few weeks after she came home

47

from the hospital. Mama was in front of me pushing the cart, when she stopped, and I accidentally stepped on the back of her shoe. She turned around, and I flinched when she scratched the end of her nose. She laughed like it was some kind of joke, and winked at me.

"You think you can manipulate me? I'll give you something to flinch over." I stood quietly and gave no response. Shaking her head, she looked back at the list.

After we unpacked the car, Mama sat out on the cement stoop in front of our house, petting our grey cat that had grown fat from his kitten days. He slowly winked his green eyes while she scratched his ears, chuckling.

Still looking at him, she said, "My cats have never disappointed me," and raised her eyebrow.

Sitting next to her was a ceramic blue bowl filled to the brim with cat food, food spilling out around the bowl. I wonder how it tastes. Mama measured every portion of the food I ate, and she became infuriated if anyone fed me without her supervision. Especially my paternal grandparents. She'd taunt me when I left for their house, "Your grandparents are going to make you fat like they are." I didn't understand why Mama was worried. I was skinny, even though she was skinnier.

We went to her friend's house for a party that weekend. I could hear her from my stool making jokes about fat people to the group of adults. Laughter erupted from the living room. I leaned back to look in the living room; the adults were sprawled on the couches with their beer bottles. I stood up quietly and snuck outside.

The bright sun made me squint as I walked to the side of the house. Overgrown bushes blocked my path, and I had to push the branches back to get to the back of the house. The back yard was a sloping hill of mowed grass. I grinned, and tucked my hands behind my head to roll down the hill like a log. When I stood up the whole yard spun around me, blue, green, brown house. In the corner of the yard I saw cherry tomatoes climbing a trellis. I ran over and snapped one off the vine and threw the red globe into my mouth. Mmmmmm! The tomato squirted seeds out onto my t-shirt. Oh No! I scraped at the tiny seeds with my fingernail so that Mama wouldn't see.

Mama never noticed because she had a special friend at the party. She introduced him to me later that night. With a crooked smile, he shook my hand, and called me, "Ma'am." I laughed, and then ran away when I caught Mama's eye.

Whenever he came over to our house he'd call out as soon as he got there, "Where's my blue eyed-angel?" and I would come running. He made me laugh one night, "Man, I'm so tired I might need toothpicks to hold open my eyelids!"

Mama gave him a dirty look. "Well you best be getting those toothpicks then, because you're not staying the night here."

On my sixth birthday I hoped he would bring me a cake covered with candy sprinkles, but instead, he brought a miniature pink sewing machine that really worked. The sewing machine was the size of a book and had a foot pedal the size of a walnut. I giggled when I saw it, completely charmed with how perfect it was.

"Oh, thank you!" I gave him a hug. "Mama look! Tiny scissors, and look at these baby spools of thread!" I wanted to tear open the box, already picturing making a blanket for Mary Jane.

Mama considered it with raised eyebrows. "Well, that's a strange toy. Don't open it," she said with a quick glanced over at her boyfriend. "We'll open it another time, when I have time to show you how it works."

It gathered dust on the top of the bookshelf for a few months where I looked at it with longing, until Mama threw it away.

I wanted her boyfriend to be my dad. One night, as he carried me half asleep from the car after a party, I wrapped my arms around his neck and murmured, "Will you be my daddy?"

With a sigh, he patted my back, and softly whispered in my ear, "I wish it were possible, blue-eyed angel. But your mama doesn't love me."

My heart sunk, I was going to lose him. Mama saw us and protested that I was a big girl and could walk by myself. She broke up with him later that night.

When it was Dad's weekend for a visit, my paternal Grandparents threw me a party with balloons and six pink candles that flickered on a big chocolate cake. The car was quiet when Dad drove me back home. He was having one of his down days, and didn't talk to me, but I didn't mind. The inside of my mouth was cut from the last slap Mama gave me. I looked out the window while he flipped through radio stations.

He pulled into my driveway, and the cats scattered in front of the car. The black cat climbed the lilac tree with her ears back, while the fat gray cat sauntered up the steps towards Mama standing on the porch. She gave Dad a steely glare when I climbed out of the car, and hurried past her into the house with my box of birthday presents. I rushed into my room to hide the toys, but Mama slammed the door shut and followed me.

"Let's see what they got you," Mama said, stopping me from shoving the toys under the bed.

I pulled out a doll that Grandma had given me, a doll that I had begged for, that ate real baby food and had dirty diapers. Guilt flooded through me, even though I didn't know why. Mama snorted in disgust.

"That is the ugliest doll I've ever seen. It's going to mold and get all gross! I can't believe they got it for you."

I agreed right away, "Yes! It is ugly!"

Her eyes considered me for a moment and lines deepened around her mouth.

"They spoil you rotten."

I took a step back away from her, holding the doll out in front of me. The space in my room felt even smaller and the air felt like it crackled with danger. She gave me an icy stare, and then turned and walked out of my room. I could hardly breathe, and my hands shook as I hurried to hide the doll away.

Soon after that, Mama met a man named Adam, the man who would one day become my stepfather. He was a tall man, with shaggy black hair, and a red mark on the back of his arm. He let me examine it, and told me the mark came from eating too many strawberries as a boy. I stared at the red mark, and pictured a little boy gluttonously sitting on a pile of strawberries with red lips and a round tummy. Later, he played in a water rivulet with me that flowed through our dirt driveway after a heavy rain. We made leaf boats and little rock dams, while Mama watched from the doorway.

Dad also came by that same weekend, and he brought me a red bike with training wheels. He walked along next to me while I rode it up the country road by our brown house. It had a beautiful bell with a thumb slide that I rang over and over. He didn't seem annoyed by its repeated metallic sound. He caught a baby snake in his bare hands nearly escaping into the grass. He held the snake curled up in his palm out for me to look at it. The snake tasted the air with its tiny flickering tongue, making me smile. I had never seen something so small that was alert and alive. I wanted to hold it, but instead he put the baby snake into a cigarette plastic wrapper and twisted closed the top. He was quiet on our walk. I tried to cheer him up by sharing the flower stories I had learned as we passed them growing on the side of the road.

Dad took me home with him that night, and I stayed with him for a week. He played pool at his pool table the entire time. We didn't talk very much; my days were filled with the clicking sounds of the pool cue shooting the balls, the squeak of the blue chalk on the stick, the clink of the balls being racked, and a growing pile of fast food containers. His house was quiet, dark, and gloomy, and I spent a lot of my time curled up in a ratty chair, watching him play. I pulled on the stuffing that had escaped from a hole, and twisted it into a spike, all while trying to convince myself not to act awkward around him. He's your Dad, not a stranger.

We rode from place to place on his motorcycle, only now I sat in the black side car. It was uncomfortable to be seated down so low, level with the passing car tires. I watched the blur of the road that flashed by mere inches away, and was tempted to reach out and run my fingers on it.

Dad took me to visit his girlfriend, Wanda, who had a house in the next town. There was a rusty, black metal spike fence that separated her yard from the sidewalk, and I climbed it and pretended I was on a pirate ship when I played outside. "Ahoy there mates! Who goes there?" I called to the leaves that cartwheeled down the street in the wind. Her house was messy when I walked inside, and the air was thick with dust motes that hung in the yellow light from the dirty windows. There were candy canes out in a dirty cup that sat on top of a dusty piano. I walked over, tempted.

"You can't eat those, hun. Those candy canes are as old as I am," Wanda said, and her eyes crinkled in the corners as she smiled. I stared at the candy canes, amazed they had made them red and white striped in those ancient times.

Wanda had wild, red hair and wore lots of blue eye shadow. At dinner time, she and Dad ate special mushrooms they had picked a few days earlier. I watched her put green tomatoes into flour, and then into a pan of oil where they snapped and sizzled. The cooked tomatoes smelled wonderful, and I tried a bite. They didn't taste as good as they smelled. Wanda glanced over at me, and laughed,

"You don't like those?"

I shook my head no.

"Aww that's too bad. I grew them myself."

I gave her a sheepish smile and got a wink in return.

"You know CeeCee, you have beautiful eyes." Wanda said, putting a piece of buttered bread on my plate. I bit into the bread, but it was hard to swallow because of the lump in my throat.

That night Dad decided we were going to stay at Wanda's house. Later, when I crawled into the musty sleeping bag, her friendly overrun house was suddenly spooky. The shelves in the room had odd trinkets that were ordinary enough when I had the lights on, but now were scary shadows glaring at me. Wanda tucked me in. Pulling the edge of the sleeping bag up under my nose, I peeped at her from the top of it.

"Awww, come here a sec," she said, and grabbed my hand, helping me off the floor. We tiptoed down the stairs past Dad snoring in the recliner, and went outside.

"Let's catch some fireflies," she said. The little lights twinkling around me. It was too dark for her to see my smile.

She posed like a statue, blue sweatpants pulled up high, and her hands suspended in the air, waiting for the fireflies to light up and show us where they were hidden. I laughed, watching her chase them. She clumsily sprang after them, and gave a deep laugh every time she captured one in her cupped hands. We filled the glass jar, and she tapped air holes into the metal lid with a nail. Wanda handed it to me.

"These little guys will keep you company. They have the power to scare off any bad guys." She smiled at me as I walked back to my room. I climbed back into my sleeping bag and fell asleep, with my hand wrapped around the jar, watching the fireflies blink their tiny lights.

After that night, I wished I could stay at her house forever.

Dad drove me to visit his parents the next day. Grandma took me swimming at her neighbor's pool. She covered her curly gray hair with a funny white rubber hat, while I sat with my legs dangling in the water on the side of the pool and blew up orange arm floaties. After sliding them up my arms I took a running jump into the water and splashed Grandma.

"CeeCee!" she screamed, her hands reaching up to check her cap. I bobbed next to her. She pushed me into the deep end. I rolled on my back and spit water, pretending to be a sea otter.

After a while I climbed out, wrapped a towel around me and walked back to Grandma's yard. The tractor was going. Grandpa was making neat stripes across the back yard. After he turned the corner he saw me and waved me over. When I got closer, he scooped me up and gave me a ride on his riding lawn mower. The steering wheel vibrated in my hands and he said, "Make sure to keep it straight."

After a few swipes I said, "Going straight is boring, Grandpa!" He laughed and let me turn circles around his fruit trees.

Then, I was hungry, so I hopped off and ran into the house. Grandma had a sandwich all ready for me, four triangles on a plate with a pile of grapes in the center.

After I finished, Grandma asked, "Want to help me make my bed?"

We tugged the blankets off, shook the pillows free from their cases, and remade the bed with fresh sheets. She showed me how she liked her corners folded.

"These are military corners. When your Grandpa was in the army, his officer would bounce a quarter off the bed. If it didn't bounce, they'd be in trouble."

I found a nickel on the dresser and threw it on the bed. It landed with a thud. Grandma laughed.

Grandma had a dresser in her bedroom that was filled with purses, white gloves and jewelry. She let me play with her purses, and I draped them around my neck and pinned on her big flower pins. She put ropes of her multi-colored round beaded necklaces on my neck, and gently clipped on the matching earrings.

"Oh, so fancy!" Grandma said.

Walking into the bathroom Grandma pulled out a wicker basket from under the sink. It was filled with little sample lipsticks with tiny clear lids. I puckered my lips and Grandma painted my lips red, then smiled at me.

"This is what you do when you put on lipstick," Grandma said, and blotted her lips. I tried it too, and we laughed at our butterfly shaped kisses left behind on the tissue.

Dad showed up a little later to take me back home. On our way there he made one last stop at his friend's house. They sat outside in their shorts on striped plastic lawn chairs and smoked cigarettes. I wandered through the garage and found a coffee can full of smelly liquid and crawling with bugs. Curious, I hit the side of the can and watched the bugs land on their backs at the bottom, and their little legs kicked. I brought it out to the men, curious.

"What is this?" I held it under Dad's nose.

"You stay away from that! What are you doing, hitting the can to watch the bugs squirm?"

"How did you know?"

They laughed. "We know everything," Dad's friend said, and sagely nodded.

There was a marked difference between Mama and him. Dad was moody, but he didn't punish me for embarrassing him. He still slapped me, and his voice became loud in an instant when he was upset. I always cowered down when he yelled, overwhelmed by his anger and the volume, not sure of when the pain was going to come. Mama rarely raised her voice; she let her hands do her talking.

I didn't see Dad for the rest of the summer. He called on the phone one night, and said he was busy picking up hot chicks at the bar. I never saw Wanda again, but in my dreams she still tucked me at night on days Mama didn't talk to me.

~ 9 ~
BLACKBERRIES

The August before I started first grade was miserably humid. I ate my breakfast and ran outside to take care of the chickens. Sweat was on my upper lip, and my shirt was already sticking to me. The sun beat on the black pump and burned me. Ow! I blew on my hands and shook them to cool them.

Mama called from the front step.

"Want to go black berry picking?"

I looked over at her. Her face was shadowed by the dark door frame, the rest of her body bright in sunlight.

"Blackberries?"

"Yes, you know, blackberries. Maybe we can make a pie." Her face came forward into the sunlight then, and her white teeth glittered.

A pie! This was such a new idea I needed a moment to think. Maybe she likes me again. The water gushed out of the pumps mouth and hit the pan. Little drops sprayed my legs.

"Yes please!"

"Finish the chickens then, and come inside." Mama continued with uncharacteristic patience.

I ran with the water pan over to the pen. The chickens pecked under my feet for bugs.

"Get out of the way, you fat old hen!" Tulips squawked and fluffed her feathers trying to fly, when I set down the water.

By the time I ran back to the house, Mama was already locking the door. She had a metal bowl in her hand and a white colander tucked under her arm.

"Get in the car."

I climbed in my spot in the back seat, and we drove off. It was Mama's new red car. She had brought it home the other day and revved it in the driveway, calling out the open window, "Check this baby out!"

We drove deep into the overgrown woods. The tree branches reached across the road and swept the sides of the car. It felt like we had been driving forever. We bumped over a rickety old bridge spanning a trickle of a stream. At the neck was a pond blocked by a beaver dam. Mama pointed out the dam. "Wow, would you look at that?" I looked at her instead, my heart pounding. Why is she acting so different?

Mama slowed down to keep our heads from hitting the roof. "Not too much further," she said, but that wasn't true. It was a lot further, and the woods were dark. There were blackberry bushes closer to town, so I wondered where the heck we were going. Finally, she pulled off into a grassy spot, the car rolling to a stop. We hadn't seen a car or house in a long time. There wasn't another soul for miles around.

She seemed nervous as she sat there for a few moments. I popped the seat forward and opened the passenger door ahead of her and jumped outside. The sun beat the scent of warm blackberries down on me.

I hitched the strap of my tank top back on to my shoulder and looked back at my mom. She had climbed out of the car and was standing with her hand on the door surveying the thick clot of blackberry bushes.

"Alright, let's go." Her voice was tight. I looked over at her curious, is she mad at me? We walked over to the hedges, grasshoppers jumping out of our way ahead of us.

Mama watched me for a few seconds. "It's so hot, would you like to take off your shoes?"

My toes wiggled at the thought, but I was surprised she asked. She's not mad. Why would she let me take my shoes off if she was mad?

"Sure!" I sat down in the grass and untied my shoes. "Where do I put them?"

She pointed to a spot and then went back to the car for her colander, slamming the door when she had it. I snuck a blackberry off the bush while I waited, warm and full of juice. The bushes buzzed with bees crawling on the blackberries.

Mama walked back and handed me a metal bowl.

"These will make a good pie, huh Mama?"

She didn't answer me, and I wondered if she'd heard.

"Won't these make a good pie, Mama?"

She made a sound, her hands busy picking berries. I tried to keep the same pace, and soon had a handful in my bowl. I didn't want to get into trouble for being slow.

Little patters came from the bushes as over-ripe berries fell to the ground. My bare toes squelched on berries, and my fingers were stained red with berry juice. Every now and then I popped one in my mouth.

Mama and I been there about ten minutes when the birds in the nearby trees sent out loud caws. The sound swelled so I turned to look. A crash of dark birds rushed into the air with flapping wings. I watched them fly in a dark rush over the tops of the trees.

The car horn blared, cutting through the sounds of the birds. Mama and I jerked and spun around to look.

Mama squinted as she stared at the car. "Someone's there." I looked hard, but didn't see anyone. The blaring horn grabbed at my insides and shook them. There was a ripple behind the windshield. Mama yelled, before I knew what it was. "Smoke!"

Finger-like tendrils of gray smoke snaked out into the hot air shimmering by the open driver's window. The delicate curls darkened as black clouds belched from the window. Smoke leaked from the crack at the bottom of the driver's side door, mixing with the black.

What's happening? I saw flickers of movement inside the car. A flash of orange licked the edge of the steering wheel. The horn still blared.

Mama jerked, her movement catching my eye. "The car's going to blow up," she mouthed, but I barely heard her over the horn. She took a few steps to the left, and spun in a circle, before throwing her blackberry bowl in the air. In that instant she ran. I stood with my bowl, frozen in place, watching her run away from me.

After a second, I followed after her, my steps slow and hesitant. Why isn't she running out to the road? Where is she going? I looked back at the burning car and saw my shoes sitting there. Reaching down, I tucked them under my arm and hurried after Mama.

She tried to weave her way through a wall of the blackberry hedge, arguing with herself, "Not this way, no this way is blocked." She wasn't talking to me. I didn't know who she was talking too.

I followed her into the hedge, but she stopped. The thorns grabbed her, twisting around her arms. She yanked at them. Spinning, she gave a vicious tug at the bush and tore herself free. She ran back out of the hedge, but I was blocking the way, caught in the thorns too.

I cried, "Mama, Mama," trying to spin the way she had, the thorns buried in my clothing and skin. She didn't look at me as she slammed into me on her way out. I was left tangled and trapped in the blackberries.

"Mama!" The roar of the fire drowned out my scream. I twisted and turned, ripping my shirt in the branches. A branch raked itself across my face. Thorns clawed at my bare belly, and grabbed my hair, blonde strands left behind when I wrenched myself free.

With my heart thudding in my ears, I wiped blood off of my face. Where was Mama? I went back in front of the car. "Mama!" The air was smoky all around me. I coughed. "Mama?" She was gone. She left me! Why did she leave me? Was I too slow? The gray smoke stung my eyes. I didn't know where to go. Tears ran down my face.

The smoke was clearer in the back of the blackberries. I stumbled over there, retching with wet coughs, and saw that there was a space that opened to a path. I pushed a few hanging branches out of the way as I followed it. The air was better here too, so I crouched down and took deep breaths. "Mama?" No answer.

She was gone.

I followed the path as it curved between the towering bushes, holding my shoes over my bowl to not lose any berries. The car crackled behind me, but the air was clearer the farther I went. On the other side of a bend, I was forced to stop. The path was blocked by a granite boulder. Mama was just reaching the top of it. I tried to climb it, only to slide off its steep side.

I gave a mighty screech, "Mama! Help me, Mama!" She jumped down without looking back. I listened, only hearing my heart pound in my ears and the trees crackling from flames. Every muscle felt weak, and I wanted to curl up on the ground and cry.

I couldn't climb over the rock with my berry bowl and shoes in my hands, but I was afraid to let them go. I remembered the whipping I got the time I left my jacket at Grandma's.

The grey smoke creeping down the path forced me into action. I dropped everything to run my hands along the granite's surface. My fingers found a slim edge, and I pulled myself up, my bare feet scrambling against the surface searching for toe holds. I reached for another groove as sweat trickled in my eyes and pulled myself higher. My foot slipped from its spot. I slid down the side, grating my palms and ripped a fingernail trying to stop. Stabbing around, my toe found an edge, stopping my fall. I froze there with my heart pounding in my throat. Taking a few deep breaths, I regained my balance and sent out my fingers to search for another ledge. Slowly, I stretched forward and pulled myself along. My elbows and knees were skinned, but I made it to the top.

Standing on the boulder, I looked out at the forest that stretched in all directions as far as I could see. Behind me, the black smoke channeled up into the blue sky through the open blackberry glade like a chimney.

I found Mama. She was still running, and she looked miniature, she was so far away.

"Mama! Mama!" I screamed as loud as I could through my hands. She hesitated for a moment, before running faster. Did she not hear me? I slid down the other side of the rock that sloped to the ground.

I couldn't see her from the ground, but ran in the direction I had seen her. Bushes blocked my way. After clearing a few I lost my sense of direction. I ran and ran, but didn't see her again. With heaving breaths, I covered my face with my hands. My nose and eyes were wet from tears.

I had lost her.

I took a deep breath and tried to stop crying. I had to keep going.

There was a flash of blue through the trees. Her shirt! I wanted to yell, but my lungs burned like fire, giving breaths that sounded like whistles. After another turn, I caught a glimpse of her again, but she dipped out of sight. I pushed slapping branches out of my way to reach her, no longer noticing my bare feet pounding over rocks or sticks. I wanted Mama.

I had been chasing her for an hour when finally, around a corner, I saw her standing in a shallow creek. She was breathing hard, bent over with her hands on her knees. I ran up to her, and she turned around slowly. She stared at me for a minute, her eyes wide with surprise. I burst into tears, so relieved to see her.

She sighed and looked away. "Ok, we're safe now, we're in the water. Let's get out of here."

We followed up the creek for a while, splashing in it because it was shallow. Mama pointed, "What's that?" A dirt road showed through the trees.

We pushed through the last of the bushes. The road felt smooth to my feet after the forest.

"I ran from you because I was panicked," Mama said.

She took another deep breath, before adding, "We are going to walk a little bit, then run a little bit." We did this for miles, long past side aches, and lungs that gasped for air.

I saw a glow of light in the woods ahead of us.

"What's that Mama?" She didn't answer. Our feet pounded against the dirt road. As we got closer I could see a window.

At the driveway, Mama lost her composure. She staggered to a tree for support. "Help us! Help us please!" she cried. I looked at her, surprised at her sudden panic, and then ran down the driveway to knock on the door. The door opened and a lady stood there flabbergasted. Mama's words tumbled out and made no sense as we bled on her front stoop.

"Where on earth did you come from?" The lady put her arm around Mama's shoulders.

She brought us into her living room where she swathed us in Band-Aids. "Oh my goodness," she said when she bandaged my torn toe nails and bloody bare feet. The lady called the fire department while Mama lay on the couch. I heard them talk about the concern of moving a fire engine over that one-hundred-year-old bridge.

By the time the fire department arrived, all that was left of the car was its metal engine and frame, and some blobs of melted glass. Even the tires had burned off. The Fire Department said they had not seen a natural fire burn so hot before. Mama was investigated for arson, and she was nervous. The police came by the next day and took a report. She didn't let them talk to me. Everyone called it a miracle that a forest fire never happened.

We didn't talk about the fire. Finally, after weeks passed, I couldn't wait any longer. "That sure was scary, huh Mama?"

Mama looked at me for a minute. "It's a good thing that you chased after me. I would have never gone back for you." Her voice sounded cold, and I shivered. I knew that I would have burned up or been lost forever in those dark woods.

~ 10 ~
THE BLUE HOUSE

It was Christmas day, and Adam, Mama's new boyfriend, was supposed to be there early that morning to celebrate with us. I jumped up and down when he arrived, excited to see him, and Mama straightened her new shirt and smiled. "Merry Christmas," she said, and gave him a hug. We had a Christmas tree with silver tinsel and blinking lights, and holiday music played in the background. I put a few pieces of tinsel on my head and twirled them around my finger, pretending I had long silvery curls, while Mama and Adam talked over mugs of coffee.

After breakfast I ran to the tree for my gifts. The first one was a dollhouse that Mama had made me out of a cardboard box. The doll house had a cardboard bed made from a cigarette box, and came with an inch high, miniature plastic person. I named him Peter. Mama also made me a Raggedy Ann doll from a kit, with black, button eyes and a red triangle for a nose. I wrapped her spindly, striped arms around my waist and hugged her for dear life. These were the first presents I remember receiving from Mama.

Besides those two presents, Mama and her boyfriend had made me a stick hobby horse out of an old broom. They gave each other secret winks and smiles when they talked about the fun they had while creating my toys. I rode around the wrapping paper with my horse and Raggedy Ann, and made galloping noises, until Mama told me to settle down.

When it was time for lunch Adam disappeared outside. He

returned after a few minutes with two full paper bags. He unpacked a big steak out of one of the bags, and placed it on the countertop while I looked at it in wonder. He pulled out potatoes, a bottle of wine, and a pumpkin pie. They cooked dinner together, giggling when they bumped into one another in the small kitchen. He poked and tickled her in the ribs, and she swatted at him with her striped dish towel. I silently watched them from my bedroom doorway with my hand covering my smile. Mama's happy now.

Mama brought my new toys over to Adam's house. She left them there so that I had something to play with when we visited on the weekend. I was sent upstairs to the spare room of Adam's house, while they stayed in the living room watching a movie and eating popcorn. Their joy was contagious, driving me to want to be included in their fun. I made a make-believe circus for them. With my tongue sticking out the side of my mouth, I carefully drew a paper lion and elephant and cut them out with my pink scissors. I prepared paper pistachio ice cream cones with sprinkles as treats, and handed out little green tickets to redeem for a ride on my fancy new stick horse.

I ran downstairs when I finished. "Hey you guys."

"Don't say guys, I'm a girl," Mama said.

I started again. "Ladies and gentlemen, I present to you, a Circus!" I handed out the tickets.

They both laughed. Mama looked at Adam. "Want to play?"

"Sure!" he said, and they got up and followed me up the white painted stairs.

At the entrance of the spare room I demanded a ticket for entrance. They walked in, and I made my horse neigh and prance around them.

Mama shook her head and said, "Kids are so funny." Adam grinned at her and hopped behind me for a horse ride. I smiled, and fireworks of joy shot through my body at their attention.

Mama's boyfriend gave me the sense that we were a real family. Mama was a different person when she was with him.

A few months after we played the circus game, we moved into Mama's boyfriend's house in Pennsylvania. But what I thought was a happy family gradually changed over the next couple weeks, as though I were a balloon drifting away from their joined hands.

This time lonely pangs hit me in a more poignant and personal way than it ever had before. I didn't understand why Adam made her happy when I never could. I was use to a silent house, now there was laughter and constant talking, except I was never included. Am I messing up their happiness? It felt wrong for me to live with them.

I promised myself, It's okay, I'll be a good girl, and Mama will want to be around me like she promised. My life was peaceful in other ways. Adam had never seen her slap my face, so I felt safe around him.

My bedroom was on the second story of Adam's little blue farm house while Mama slept down stairs in Adam's bedroom. I walked into my room, and saw there were two beds to jump on. In the corner sat an old fashioned baby buggy with bouncy springs. Where did the little girl go who had left it behind? The room had warm sunshine spilling across the floor, and I curled up on my bed to read a book about garden fairies. After finishing the book, I ran outside to peep under the purple garden flower heads for any hidden fairies. It was a magical time, and I expected to see a tiny face peeping back at me.

Mama and Adam left for the store. They were gone for hours, and the house felt creepy. I left my room and went to the living room to wait. There was a dime on the coffee table. I picked it up, and dragged it across the top. The wood dented in a fun way. I got excited, and drew a tic-tac-toe board, smiling as the wood gave way under the light pressure. I tried to win against myself, but I tied. Cat's game! I tried again.

Mama came home and walked into the living room, setting her bags down on the end of the couch. Her eyes focused on the table and me sitting there still holding the dime, and her face flushed dark red. A chill ran down my back. What have I done?

"I trusted you to be alone for a short while, and you ruined Adam's table." She balled her hands at her sides. "He made that!" Adam had slipped in behind her and nodded his shaggy head in agreement.

"I'm sorry, Mama," I whispered, twisting the front of my shirt with my hands. Adam didn't think I was a good girl any more, even though I had tried. He saw the monster in me.

From that moment on, Mama's nice voice was gone, and the wooden spoon was back harder than ever. The house was cordoned off to their side, and my room. During the day Mama said, "Stay outside."

There was a boy named Johnny who lived down the road from our blue house who was seven like I was, and became my best friend. He had an amazing Star Wars play set, with all the little action figures, and a real Chewbacca stuffed doll. We always fought over who got to play Han Solo, and who had to play Luke.

That day, I wouldn't give Han Solo back.

Johnny said, "Just forget it, my stuff is getting dirty."

He grabbed his toys off the grass and brought them back into the house, skipping out a minute later holding a popsicle. He knew I couldn't have any. Mama had told me before I went down there, "I'm friends with his mom, I'll find out."

We walked to the backyard. He bit chunks out of the orange popsicle and crunched on them extra loud. I was getting mad, but wouldn't give him the satisfaction of saying anything. His dad was using a chop saw, piling fresh yellow boards by the back deck. There was a pile of gray boards stacked under the pine trees that Johnny's dad said we could have.

"Watch out for rusty nails!"

We dragged the boards deep into the trees, and made a club house. Johnny wouldn't let me use the hammer because I was a girl. I threw a pinecone hard at his back, and he laughed. Instead, I searched for flat logs that we used as table and chairs, and broad pieces of bark to use for plates. We pretended we were prospectors looking for gold, finishing our base camp.

While searching for gold out in the back woods, we discovered a clay bank. The red clay was easy to dig out with our fingers, and we chattered in excitement about selling it. Who wouldn't want to buy the soft clay that rolled up so nicely into balls? As the pile of clay grew, our topic changed to what we wanted to buy with our money after we sold it. Johnny wanted a race car, and I wanted a pony.

We made clay marbles, and dried them in the sunshine on the hot asphalt road. After they dried, we chose the ones with the least cracks and raced them down the road to see which marble rolled the farthest. The clay was also perfect for me to squish and form into tiny bowls and plates. I baked them in the sun for my flower fairies.

Johnny came over one rainy day while his mom left for the store. We raced upstairs to my bedroom. It was the first time he had been in my house, and he gazed around my bare room with his eyebrows up. He pushed the baby carriage back and forth with one finger and then bent down to examine the springs. He looked over at me with a bored expression, the freckles standing out on his nose like cinnamon sprinkled on eggnog. I shrugged my shoulders in a weak apology. "Well, what do you want to do?"

A game evolved into us playing house. He was the daddy and I was the mommy, and we spoke to each other in made up voices.

"When are we going to clean the house for the baby?" I warbled in a high pitched voice.

He answered, in a deep, gruff voice, "I don't know, I have to go to work." He pretended to be at work and stomped around my room, while I hummed a silly high pitched tune, and cleaned air dishes. And in an instant, the whole day had passed in, and Johnny opened the pretend front door, "Honey, I'm home!"

We ate a pretend dinner, and had pretend arguments. We competed with one another as we tried to come up with the more interesting story line, telling each other what to say and do. At one point, we both lay down on my bed, fully clothed, and he told me to roll on top of him. Right at that instant, my door was flung open as Mama stormed in.

She gasped and screamed, "What are you doing?"

We scrambled apart, I wasn't sure what we had done, but we both knew we were in trouble. "Out!" Mama's eyes narrowed into slits, and we ran for the door. Mama moved to block me in the doorway, and leaned down close to my face. With her lip curled she said, "You just think you're so smart. Say that you are smart. Say it! Go on, say it!"

I was confused, so I mumbled, "I'm smart."

Mama slapped me hard across the face. I stumbled against the door frame, my face scratched by her finger nails.

"How dare you backtalk me," Mama hissed, and then she spun away and stamped down the stairs. Johnny stood there staring, his mouth hanging open. I looked away, so humiliated that he saw Mama hit me. He slunk down the stairs and ran home to wait for his mom.

He didn't come back over to play for a few weeks. I didn't know if he wanted to be friends anymore. I didn't understand what we had done wrong, and there were no explanations given.

I tried to have fun playing outside by myself. I dug in the red clay bank and talked about my dreams, like Johnny was there listening to me. Inside my heart was a horrible ache. I dropped the clay back to the ground rather than work it into marbles. After brushing myself off, I sat at the end of my driveway staring down the road towards his house, wishing he would come.

I saw him walk up the road, his blue baseball cap pulled low over his eyes. I couldn't help but laugh as I jumped up and ran down towards him. When he saw me running, he ran too, both of us stopping a few feet apart and smiled. We didn't talk about what happened, instead darted out into the woods to our club house, and began prospecting for gold again.

Another neighbor boy from up the hill joined us, and we all played with little cars in the dirt. The two boys kept involving my car in their horrible car accidents. I was indignant.

"Hey! My car is trying to get to the mountains for a picnic! Stop smashing it!"

For my seventh birthday, Mama and Adam gave me a white rabbit, and I spent the entire summer in trouble because of her. I named her Princess, because she was so beautiful. She sat on my lap while I hummed a little song, running my fingers through her soft fur.

"Sweet, sweet bunny, beautiful bunny. Love you, love you, love you Honey."

Adam fenced in a small patch of dirt with chicken wire for her out by their vegetable garden, and out of sight. I forgot to feed Princess one night, and Mama yelled at me in front of Adam. I felt so bad I couldn't look at Adam.

"How is it possible for you to eat your dinner, when you didn't feed poor Princess? I hope she starves to death so you can see how you made her suffer by being so neglectful."

I couldn't understand what was wrong with me that I forgot to feed her. It happened over and over again, until every time I saw the bunny I filled with nausea and dread.

Mama yelled at me, even after I fed her. "She's digging CeeCee. She's so desperate for food and attention that she burrowed in the dirt to get to the garden. Wow!"

It seemed every night when I was allowed to come back inside, Adam and Mama were waiting for me at the door. I wanted to run as soon as I saw them.

"We've been watching you for the last few hours," Mama said. "We wanted to see if you'd ever go check on your poor bunny. And you didn't. We knew you'd forget." Mama laughed, and shook her head. "I can't believe I ever trusted you. I'm disgusted. You don't deserve her."

Tears ran down my face, "I'm trying Mama!"

"You don't try, you do it."

Soon after the school year began, they gave her away to a girl while I was in science class. I looked at her empty cage, and cried. Mama said the new owner was a better girl than me, and would take care of the bunny.

A few days later, I discovered that we were about to move out of state.

I had overheard Mama talk to Adam after dinner that we would be moving to Arizona at the end of the month. Mama wanted to follow her parents, who had moved there six months earlier.

Dad and his girlfriend took me out for pizza so that they could talk to me about the move. Dad shared that Mama taking me out of state was illegal, and that Mama was a criminal.

"I'm sick of her always taking you away from me! She knows this hurts me." He rubbed his palm over his face, and then made me practice, over and over, how to make a collect call on the telephone. He played the operator, as his girlfriend nodded solemnly, and stuffed the corner of a piece of the greasy pizza into her mouth.

"Your Dad loves you," she said.

Dad had wet eyes when we hugged goodbye. He dropped me back off at home, and I felt muddled, and tired.

Mama laughed when I told her Dad cried. "Serves him right. Let's see him try to stop me. What an evil man." Two days later, she said I was just like him.

The house became a bustle of chaos as Mama packed. I tripped over boxes that were stacked in every room, and couldn't find anything I needed. Adam marked the boxes with a black marker, and Mama tore packing tape off with her teeth to seal them. She gave me a cardboard apple box. "Pack all your belongings in here. Be choosy, because whatever doesn't fit isn't coming with us."

We had a huge yard sale, and while the sale was going on I played in the creek with the Smith kids.

"Watch out for the leeches!" my friend's parents warned us.

What are leeches? My friends and I laughed as we splashed up and down the creek, looking for leeches. We didn't find any, but we did find an angry crawdad that came out from under a rock snapping at our stick. We squealed and poked at him until he disappeared down an underwater hole on the side of the bank.

When I returned to the house, I saw that the entirety of what was left over from the sale had been tossed into the back of a truck to be taken to the dump. I cried out when I saw my baby carriage buried under a pile of black garbage bags, one wheel spinning, along with my stick horse and doll house.

Mama said, "It's gone, you don't need it."

I was glad that Peter, my miniature figurine, was small and fit inside my box.

Johnny didn't come over to say goodbye, but the boy up the street came down and gave me his mom's mouse pin with one pink sparkly eye.

"Remember me," he said.

I accepted it awkwardly and wished it was from Johnny. I was hurt and bewildered that Johnny didn't come say goodbye.

Adam and Mama bought a new car to take us to Arizona, a shiny penny colored two-door Honda. When it was time to leave the sales lady opened the door, and I climbed into the back seat by stepping on the front seat.

Mama wiped at the front seat, sweeping hard at dirt that wasn't there. She had her nice smile on when she said goodbye to the sales lady. Fear raised its biting head inside of me. I didn't want her to get in the car.

She shut her door, and Adam drove off the lot. Mama turned around in her seat, her smile replaced with ugly lines. "How could you do that? The sales lady thought you were disgusting that you would do such a shameful thing. It's a brand new car." Her eyes were hot on me and I didn't dare move, in case that activated her hand. She continued, "You made it dirty. A brand new car and you already made it dirty."

Every time I climbed out of the car, I regretted that first step. My shoe had branded the front seat with my dirt. For years, Mama told the story to anyone who would listen, about how I stepped on the front seat of a brand new car.

We camped at KOAs each night as we traveled through the states down to Arizona. Mama and her boyfriend were occupied with each other, hugging, and holding hands, and laughing together. I wandered all over the different campgrounds.

Watching other families fascinated me, even though it made me feel more alone. I stood on the outskirts of the camp sites, trying to stay unnoticed. The smell of cooked hamburgers and hotdogs made my mouth water. No one noticed a scrawny seven year old, with dusty toes that hung over the tops of her sandals, and tight clothing. There was a dad who laughed with his children when they returned from swimming. They were wrapped in striped towels with wet hair that stuck up in all directions. I saw a mom juggle her fussy baby on her hip while the baby reached out for a bag of potato chips. Her two preschoolers jumped up and down, and clamored for the food piled on the picnic table.

She said, "Ok guys, give me a sec."

Another family gathered around their camp fire in lawn chairs, with marshmallows stuck on sticks.

My family was different. If I could be a good girl, I could fix it. I meandered back to my camp where an uncooked hot dog waited for me in the cooler for dinner.

For the first few months in Arizona we lived with Adam's childhood friend, Jeff. It was strange to live there, Mama tried to be "on" whenever she was around Jeff, acting interested in me, but as soon as Jeff left the room she stopped talking as though she had been unplugged.

I was enrolled into second grade and, for the first time ever, I was an ethnic minority. I worried that the other kids wouldn't like me-- Mama was very prejudiced and always made comments-- but when we stood up to say the pledge of allegiance one of the girls beckoned me over. I skipped over to her and admired her new bracelet. After that first day it didn't seem as different as I expected.

After school I had to walk home. The morning walk to school felt adventurous and fun, but things looked different now. Was I supposed to take a left at the last street? Where was the church I passed this morning? The adobe houses all appeared the same, with their long chains of dried red peppers that swayed by their door. The air smelled spicy from the hanging peppers, and seasoned meat from family dinners. I walked quicker. At the end of the street I'll see where I am. My heart pounded when I got to the corner. I turned in circles, not sure which way I should go. I'm lost! I'm lost! I didn't know our phone number. I started to run.

There was a woman standing at the end of her driveway gathering her mail from the mail box. Somehow, by a miracle, she showed me the way home. I was crying when I burst through the front door, over an hour late. Mama was surprised. She didn't notice I was missing.

She shrugged, "Well, you'll pay better attention next time."

I set my books down in my room and then hurried over next door to my friend's. She was a year younger than me, with long brown braids. When she came to the door she held an extra set of red buckle roller skates. She handed them to me as we walked to the edge of the sidewalk. While we strapped the plastic roller skates over our shoes, I told her what happened on the way home.

"I've never walked home by myself. My mom always drives me," she said.

I considered that for a minute. I wanted her mom to drive me too, but knew what Mama would say.

We talked about what skating game to play.

"Circus?"

"No! Ballerinas!"

My friend stood up and showed me how she thought a ballerina would skate. She roller-skated in a slow circle while balanced on one leg with her arms flung out. I wobbled when I tried to circle, so I skated in a straight line, holding my hands above my head in a ring, while my skates went "bump-bump!" over the cracks in the sidewalk.

Afterwards, we sat in the shade of a tree and played hand games, clapping our hands together in perfect time as we sang 'Miss Mary Mack!' or, 'Say! Say! Oh Playmate.' She had a giant chalk collection, so we drew tic-tac-toes, funny cartoon characters, and hopscotch, wiping the chalk dust from our hands onto our shorts. She made me a chalk drawing in a pretty blue frame, and I hung it on my wall. Whenever we moved again, it went first in my cardboard box, next to Peter.

Sometime, soon after we arrived in Phoenix, we visited Grandparent's house (on Mama's side) for a few weeks. Mama and Grandma were in the kitchen getting dinner prepared, while I watched Mutual of Omaha's Wild Kingdom with Grandpa in the living room. He studied me for a minute, and smiled when I met his eyes. He waved me over to sit on his lap. I skipped across the living room and climbed up into his lap. He tickled my back as we watched the lion roar and chase a gazelle. Just as the lion attacked, his hands crept to my front. My eyes flew open and I pulled my arms tight to my sides. Maybe he did it by accident.

He did it again, and I whimpered. He whispered in my ear that if I want to be special to him and have his love, I needed to let Grandpa tickle. What am I doing wrong that he is doing this to me?

Every night I hoped he'd forget, but he always called me over. I barely breathed, trying not to cry. Mama and Grandma laughed in the kitchen as the dishes clattered, and I sat frozen on Grandpa's lap while he worked his fingers under my pinned arms.

Mama came around the corner and saw me sitting there. "Oh, you are so spoiled, CeeCee. Such a Grandpa's girl!"

Grandpa smiled at her, "Yes, she is very special to me." I was caught between the two as they stared at each other, and Mama walked out of the room.

The next morning Mama, Adam, and Grandma set off for a day of shopping, and I was left behind with Grandpa. Mama and Grandpa smiled at each other before she shut the door. The house was quiet after they left. He walked over to me, and sat down on the creaking leather couch and put his hand on my knee. He said he loved me, and I was going to learn to play fun games with him. "You are my favorite grandchild. You want to be a good girl, don't you? You do as I say, and you will be a good girl."

That night I climbed out of bed, and found Mama taking her makeup off in her room. My hands twisted together, sweaty palms and white knuckles, and I tried to tell her what happened. Her face was shiny from lotion, and she waved a Kleenex at me.

"Stop, stop. I don't want to hear anymore."

There was no way out, there was no escape. I was trapped in the car on the ice all over again.

During that visit, Grandpa killed a rattlesnake in the yard with a shovel one night. The sun was setting behind the horizon, and we watched his black shadow form ferociously chop down from the back deck. Mama clapped her hands as though he were a hero.

That same night, Grandma brought me into her room and taught me the Lord's Prayer. She repeated it over and over until I had it memorized, her finger dragging along the words written in red in the bible. She gave me a white cross with a crucified Jesus contorted painfully on it.

I frowned and said, "He looks different than in my bible picture."

Grandma ran her thumb over the smooth cross, and said, "The cross is special and made of elephant tusk. This is Jesus. His eyes are always on us."

"Always on us?" I said, and my stomach knotted.

That night I studied the man on the cross by the moonlight coming through the lace curtain window. A tear slipped down my cheek, and I whispered, "I'm sorry Jesus. I'm trying."

~ 11 ~
THE ADOBE HOUSE

During the months that we lived in Phoenix Mama continued to look for a house to buy. They searched all around the city with a realtor.

One Saturday we drove an hour into the desert to see a new listing. The realtor insisted that Mama and Adam would love it. "It's priced well under your budget, because, sadly, the owner died in the home."

The house was a brown adobe, still furnished with all his old furniture and belongings. I peeked through the door at a piano in the corner with interest. There was also a pair of blue jeans wadded up by the front door.

Mama told me to stay outside while they toured the house. I discovered a container of bleach with a weathered green label that sat tilted in the sand. Standing next to it, I scanned the horizon, and as far as I could see there was nothing but sand, and more sand, and a few rolling tumbleweeds. I pictured the three of us living there; where I would go if I needed a hiding place? Goosebumps went up my arms, I'd be like the bleach container, fully visible and exposed to Mama's critical eye.

On our way back to the car the realtor told my parents, "You know, they say there are ghosts living inside the home." My ears perked up. I was thankful my parents turned that house down, along with another one that had a yard filled with old rusty cars and trucks.

In one strange city, my parents pulled over and told me to get out of the car. I scrambled out from the back seat, and quickly scanned up and down the empty street. There was a jungle gym in the middle of an empty city lot, and as the car drove away Mama yelled out the opened car window, "Go play, we will be back in a while." They didn't return for a few hours. I waited for them, hanging upside down from the hot metal monkey bars.

Around my eighth birthday, we were shown an adobe house in the town of Casa del Fuego. I stayed outside in the dusty front yard while the realtor gave my parents the tour. Seeing a little bit of shade, I walked over and sat on the porch steps, and stared out at the cramped front yard full of dead grass. Reaching down without a thought, my hands found little clods of dirt and crumpled them into dust. I was disgusted to see that the lawn was covered in hundreds of piles of white dog poop. Inside the house, my parents were signing papers. I would soon be spending hours in the hot sun chipping them out of the grass.

We never did grow grass there, and eventually the straw-like stubble blew away in the desert wind. We didn't use the front yard anyway. Adam built a tall privacy fence around an eight by eight foot cement patio in the back yard where they spent their evenings smoking cigarettes in lawn chairs.

There was a home-made swing that hung off a pole in the middle of the yard that was left by the previous owners.

I loved my swing, and daydreamed it was a rocket ship, or a covered wagon going west, or a mom rocking me as a baby. I swung it in dizzy circles, and whipped myself around the pole as though I were a tether ball. At night I swung gently, and leaned back as far as possible while hanging on with one hand, gazing up at the stars.

At the end of our first month there, I heard the roar of a chain saw as it started up. Adam decided that the swing made the back yard look cluttered and cut down the pole. From the corner of the house I watched my swing shudder and fall over, flinching as it took my daydreams with it when it toppled.

My bedroom in the adobe house was in what used to be the back porch. One night, I heard a scurry up the side of the wall, so I jumped out of bed and flipped on the light. The raspy sound was a centipede crawling up the stucco paint. My heart thumped in my throat as it moved in fast spurts. I bent down and felt around for my shoe. When I ran over, my shadow fell across the bug. It curled up and dropped on the bed, immediately lost in the wrinkled sheets. I let out a shriek.

"What's the matter?" I heard Mama from her bedroom.

"A centipede just fell in my bed! I can't find it!" There was no noise for a minute. There was mumbling through the heater vent in the wall from their room. Finally, Mama yelled, "Just go back to bed. It's probably fine."

I stared toward their room for a moment, before ripping back the covers---nothing. Dragging the bed from the wall, I peered down the side. It wasn't anywhere. I sat there and tried to catch my breath, and then shook out my blankets. I didn't want to turn out the light, but once I did I bounded across the floor in two steps, and landed on my bed with a jump. After tucking the blankets in tight around me, I tried to sleep.

My bedroom had three large windows in the inner wall that looked into the kitchen, left over from the days when it had once been a porch. Mama hung curtains on her side of the windows. She stood there with a corner of the curtain flipped up and watched me. I never knew when she would be there. Sometimes I'd get a prickly feeling down my back and turn to look, and there would be her eyes staring from under the turned-up curtain.

"I like to watch to see if you are misbehaving," she said.

I had to be careful getting my toys off their shelf, because she might consider my room a mess. I peeked over my shoulder at her window while playing with my doll.

Mama was stricter than she ever had been before. I had more rules to obey, and I was always being punished. She slapped my face if I forgot to call Adam, "Papa."

"I said Papa that time, I promise." I cried.

"Don't lie to me, I heard you say Adam."

She used wooden spoons on my bare skin, and hit me until I lost control of myself from the pain. I'd struggle to get away, and the blows landed on my legs and back, leaving red spoon shaped welts that didn't go away.

One day, she invited Adam into my room to watch her punish me.

"Please don't make me," I cried, and she wrenched my arm and forced me to bend. My sobs came from a deeper place than pain could reach, as he stood there and watched her hit me. I fell off the bed, and tried to hide my nakedness from him.

The new house was still divided into the adult side, and my room, but Mama didn't allow me in my room during the day. I learned to love the desert. I watched for dust devils when it was windy outside, because those mini tornados were strong enough to carry away someone my size. I was supposed to watch for rattlesnakes, but always forgot as I skipped through the dust in my sandals and kicked at the tumbleweeds.

My skin wasn't use to the hot desert sun. I sunburned around my tank top, the skin on my face and shoulders turning a deep, angry red. Mama took me to the doctor when the blisters began to form. He walked into the examining room, took one look at my face, and turned to Mama. "Wow! What happened?"

I hunched in misery on the paper cover table, not sure of what kind of trouble I was in.

Mama said, "Oh I tell her to put sunscreen on, but you know kids. She was only outside for twenty minutes."

The doctor studied her for a moment and solemnly said, "This can never happen again. She has the worst sunburn I've ever seen. She might even scar. With blonde hair like that, your daughter can't be outside without sunscreen. Her skin is too fair."

He prescribed some medicine and lotions, and sent me home. I still stayed outside, but spent more time in the shade of the porch. And, as I healed my skin peeled off in sheets.

I was soon exploring the town. Men leered at me from their doorsteps, and called to me in their language, but I learned to look the other way.

One day, I noticed my shoes left leaf prints in the dust, and I looked back to see the little leaves following me, enchanted. I found a rock to kick, and after kicking the rock for a while, looked up to discover I was in a strange neighborhood. Striped blankets hung where the doors should have been, and faces peered at me out of windows before settling back into the dark gloom. Panic stopped me in my tracks, because I couldn't remember my way home. I spun around and tried to follow my footprints back, looking for the landmarks of the melted adobe building that I had passed. When I finally saw something familiar I let out a huge sigh of relief, like I'd escaped back into the sunshine.

Casa del Fuego was a small town with only a few other white

families. My family was not liked, and I wasn't sure why. I stood out among the town's people with my blonde hair and blue eyes, and school wasn't fun. The kids teased me without mercy.

"Hey Gringo! What are you doing here? Wait until we get you outside!"

I hid during recess, but my third grade teacher found me waiting along the back row of the school library, and sent me out to the play yard. It was as if the teacher had thrown a bone to wolves as the kids gathered around my gangly form. The boys and girls spoke in rapid Spanish and laughed, and I couldn't understand what they were saying. I spun in a circle and looked for an escape, but all I saw were dark eyes and mocking faces that closed in.

One of the boys entered the circle with me. He shrugged his shoulders and, with a smirk, pushed me with big, sweaty hands.

"Hey Gringo, why are you here? Why did you come? We don't want you! Why are you crying?" I backed away, but hands from behind shoved me towards him. He knocked me down. All the kids hooted as I lay on my back in the dust. The bell rang. I lay there until the kids walked away, and then got up and brushed myself off. I wiped the dirty tear marks off my face, tucked my shirt back into my pants and returned to class.

I had two friends at the school, a brother and sister whose parents owned the local restaurant, and the three of us ruled the corner where the restaurant was located. The sister was seven, a year younger than me, and the brother was ten. We raced up and down the street, and pretended our banged up bikes were wild mustangs, and played rodeo. We used flat dried Horny Toad lizards that had been run over by cars as our barrels when we ran the figure eights.

The three of us liked to spin lazy circles outside the haunted, deserted old hotel, with its front saloon doors hanging askew.

One of us would tell a story. "It's true! That one cowboy turned into an old ghost. He stomps around the hotel at night in his boots. If you're real quiet, you can hear his spurs hit the floor." Another one of us would add that if the ghost caught you, he'd run bony cold fingers across the back of your neck, and drag you down into the dark underworld. We would shake with delighted shivers, and soon dare each other to go yell "Boo!" at the ghost. None of us were that brave, so we'd creep up the steps together. We'd push open the hotel's broken saloon doors for a quick look inside. There was a dark hole in the hotel floor, faded rose colored wall paper that peeled in long curly strips, and a staircase that tilted crazily away from the wall. Right away, one of us would hear a creak that had us all sprinting for the safety of the street.

One day, as I pushed my bike from behind our house, Mama hollered at me out the window to go wash her car. I was crabby when I headed back outside with the bucket of soapy water. There were hours of work ahead of me. I thought jealously of my friends riding their bikes. Soon, my shorts were soaked from washing one side of the car. I worked on the other, sloshing the white bubbles up the side of the car with my sponge. I didn't know that Mama was standing at the window watching me when I mumbled, "This stinks."

The screen door banged, and Mama raced around the side of the house with her hair streaming behind, her eyes wild and crazy. She held her largest wooden spoon over her head. I cringed, bad pain was coming. THWACK! Mama swung it with all her strength, breaking the spoon across my face. She knocked me to the ground with the blow. I lay there dazed, seeing black out of my right eye. The sky and ground whirled. I tasted blood. My eye and cheek started to swell. I stayed on the ground trying not to make a sound, but little moans escaped. Mama stepped around me, her feet close to my head. I vaguely heard her through a ringing ear.

"YOU will clean this car with no sass."

She went back inside the house. I rolled over on to my hands and knees, and slowly stood up, wanting to retch as the world spun. Fire shot through the right side of my jaw when I tried to open my mouth. I didn't know what to do about that. Through the throbbing pain I worried that my neighbors thought I was a bad girl. I picked up the sponge from where it had landed a few feet away and finished washing the car.

When I was done, I put the bucket away in the little shed and then walked inside to find Mama. I stood quiet before her as she worked on her embroidery, until she looked up.

"I'm sorry, Mama." She blinked at me. I took a deep breath and said, "My mouth won't open right."

She gave a small laugh. "You're lucky the spoon broke, because I wasn't finished. I guess its soup for you for dinner then. Hope it's better tomorrow!"

The next morning, I leaned against the bathroom counter and

studied the mirror. My fingers traced the deep black bruise that covered the right side of my face. I covered my eyes with my hands, wishing I could hide forever. The toothbrush stayed in the water glass on the counter. I couldn't open my mouth wide enough to slide the brush in. Mama ignored me while I got ready for school; I felt like a ghost to her again.

Face flushed, I ducked my head as I made my way down the busy hallway at school. Everyone stared when I entered the classroom. The quiet exploded into whispers. I saw them laugh, and hot tears stung my eyes. Throughout the day a few of my teachers came up and asked me what had happened. I gave a tiny smile and said, "I tripped and fell into a door knob in the middle of the night." The tightness in my chest lessened when I saw that the explanation satisfied them.

I told Mama that afternoon how the teachers had questioned me about my face, and how I had lied to defend her. I thought Mama would be proud of me, and she would see that I sincerely loved her. Instead Mama was indignant. She lit her cigarette, and exhaled the smoke in a gray stream, and then said, "You better have lied. You deserved it. You won't be sassing me anymore, will you?"

The bruise lasted for a long, long time. I had to be very gentle when opening my mouth, because it hurt so much.

After the bruise faded, Mama surprised me by showing up at my school during lunch time. She pulled out two pink snowball cupcakes from a paper bag for us to share. I held the treat in my hand in awe.

Mama smiled at me, "How was your day honey?"

My heart so filled with joy that I thought I might die. I blinked back tears and smiled at her. I didn't know how to talk with her; she was so beautiful and perfect. Let the other kids make fun of me; they didn't have their moms giving them snowballs at lunch. Mama said hello to the principal on her way out.

That weekend I was surprised even further when Mama offered to take me roller skating. She drove me a few blocks over to the main street of Casa del Fuego where I roller-skated on the sidewalk right in front of the Post Office. Her arm firmly gripped mine as she guided me up the sidewalk, and then back down again a few times.

"Slow and steady, there you go!" She carefully led me around two old ladies who stood outside the post office door.

One of the ladies said to the other, "Isn't that sweet," and nodded in my direction.

Adam took a picture, and then we left. When we got home Mama disappeared inside, and life continued like it had never happened.

The principal came over for dinner one night, and Mama made a roast with potatoes. We sat around the kitchen table as the principal told a story about a difficult kid at school.

"You tell us if you catch CeeCee doing anything naughty. She's a sneak, and likes to argue. Kids these days need to be whipped into shape. You see her do something, you have my permission to hit her. Make her scared of you." Mama slapped her hand for emphasis.

His eyes flicked over at me from across the table, his bald head shining. "I'll keep my eye on her." I crept to my room. His eyes seemed to burn into me every day afterward, from where he stood watching along the walls of the school.

I always felt hungry while at school. Every day coffee cans were loaded with peanuts and kept out on the cafeteria counters for the students. I stuffed my pockets, and ate them all day long savoring their salty, oily crunch. I always waited for the moments the Principal was not looking in my direction before grabbing a handful. I didn't bring any home. I didn't want Mama to smell peanuts on my breath.

The semester ended, and it was time for my third grade parent/teacher conferences. Mama made me come with them. Adam pulled the car up to the school, and she turned to look in the back seat.

"I wonder what this teacher thinks of you. She knows who you are. Hope I don't get a bad report." She gave me a sarcastic smile, and said, "Come on Adam, this will be fun."

I shrank into the corner of the back seat. They were gone a long time. I squirmed to get comfortable, needing to use the bathroom, but didn't dare leave. The sun set and then the moon came out, and still they didn't return.

My grades were good, but I still imagined Mama getting angrier and angrier at something the teacher was saying about me. I groaned. Maybe the Principal is there too, what would he say? I closed my eyes, I could see Mama agreeing with the teacher, while the other children's parents watched and nodded. "That CeeCee, she is such trouble." I wanted to throw up and leaned my head against the car door.

Hours passed before they returned, ignoring me when they got back into the car. I watched their body language, afraid to make eye contact with them. They didn't say a word to me on the home. What does this mean? Are they really mad? My heart pounded. We pulled into the driveway. Silently, they got out and walked inside. I had to use the bathroom badly, but stayed there, my hand frozen on the door handle. After a minute I followed them, and ran for the bathroom, expecting to hear a scream from the living room. "Get the spoon!" There was nothing. That night in bed I watched the curtain, waiting for it to flip up.

The next day the school conference still wasn't brought up, and I began to relax. Mama was in the living room working on a doll. She gave it to me a few weeks later for my ninth birthday. Mama loved to make crafts, and this was the second doll I had received from her that year. My dolls were proof that Mama loved me. They were my babies, and I wiped their cloth faces and told them they were beautiful. I played only with them so that Mama might see how much I appreciated her gifts.

My dad in Pennsylvania sent a book for my birthday. He had taped money in between the pages of the book as a surprise. Filled with excitement, I jammed the handful of bills into my corduroy jeans pocket, and ran out to check the different stores for a prize that might possibly please Mama. And I finally found it! A fruit tray! She will love this! I raced home, my sandals pounding up dust clouds in my hurry to get home. I burst into the house, and found her sitting in the living room, another sewing craft laid out on the coffee table. Mama finished threading her needle and looked up. I handed it to her with my face beaming. Her eyes lit up for a second as she reached for it.

"Oh, thank you."

My heart squeezed with joy.

The gift only brought me relief for a few moments. Life continued to get harder. The pressure of having to comply with so many rules in order to avoid being hurt or insulted, or have my meals taken away was making me exhausted, and dark circles puddled under my eyes. On top of the rules, I had to keep secret everything about my home life, especially from Dad in Pennsylvania. There were the lies to remember about how clumsy I was to get my bruises, and how active I was to be so skinny. And then there was the secret within my secret life. One I couldn't acknowledge myself; Grandpa's games and his constant groping hands.

My life was like trying to navigate around hidden land mines while I waited for the explosion. One day, in frustration I pulled out a couple strands of my hair. I studied the blonde hair entwined in my fingers, and the weight in my chest felt lighter. I pulled out more of my hair, and relief flooded through me. With my pulse pounding in my throat I watched for my bedroom curtain to twitch, and prayed that Mama wouldn't catch me as I hid the loose hair under my bed.

This was a dark period in my life, but the darkest time was fast approaching.

~ 12 ~
# THE DARK HOUSE

Casa del Fuego never welcomed Adam and Mama. The locals talked fast and laughed whenever my parents passed by. I'd look back, wondering what the joke was, but their dark eyes only snapped with dirty humor and scorn.

It was two o'clock in the morning when we received a phone call that jolted us all awake. Adam cleared his throat thick with sleep, and answered, "Hello?"

My feet hit the cold floor as I scrambled out of bed and ran to the hallway to hear. A harsh male voice echoed through the receiver, "We will kill you and your family! We will grab your wife and your little girl, and drop them down the old mine shaft! No one will ever find them! Leave now, Gringo!"

My stepdad was stunned into silence, as the phone clicked off. He slowly returned the receiver to its cradle, his forehead wrinkling. He didn't see me, standing like a ghost in my pale nightgown at the end of the dark hallway. He turned to answer Mama, who was calling from the bedroom.

I knew Mama and Adam were concerned, because their worried tones carried through the heater vent in the wall. But, it didn't hinder me from continuing to explore the streets as I pleased. We lived there for two more years, despite receiving three or four more sleep jarring phone calls.

One morning we found our cat twisted in the barbed wire fence at the end of our property, dead. I held my hands over my wet eyes and pushed my palms against my eye sockets causing stars. Adam buried the cat while Mama sobbed, and then ran to her room to hide.

That week they decided it was time to leave.

Our adobe house sold a week after it was put on the market. Adam and Mama went down to the court house and eloped. The next week, Adam took a U-Haul, packed with all of our belongings, and drove it to Montana to start his new job. Mama and I stayed behind in a little rental house in Casa del Fuego so that I could finish the last month of fourth grade.

Mama softened right after Adam left. She looked over at me sitting in the passenger seat on our way to the grocery store.

"I'm counting on you, CeeCee. I hate being here alone." I shivered with happiness, because it reminded me of when I took care of her when I was five. We ran errands, and had dinner together every night.

A padded envelope arrived one day in the afternoon mail. Mama tore into it with giddy laughter and pulled out a tiny, velvet jewelry box that opened to reveal a late engagement ring. I gasped when she slid the sparkling ring down her finger; it was like a snip of the clearest icicle. Mama held it up to the sunlight, and we giggled at the tiny rainbows it made. She flashed her rainbows around the room while I chased after them to catch one in my hand. It was the first diamond I'd ever seen.

This peaceful time was the eye of the hurricane in my life.

We took an airplane out to Billings right after my tenth birthday. Mama gestured for me to look out the tiny airplane window she sat next to.

"Check out those lights," she murmured, as we flew over the city.

"They're beautiful," I whispered in awe as I leaned over, mesmerized at what seemed like a million sparkling jewels spilt across black velvet. She nodded, satisfied, and I sat back in my chair. We didn't talk for the rest of the flight.

Adam was waiting to pick us up at the Billings airport. As soon as Mama saw him, she disconnected from me, and ran into his arms for a long hug. Her eyes narrowed into slits when Adam greeted me by putting his arm around my shoulders.

We drove for about an hour down the highway, away from the

city lights. I looked out the window, but there was nothing to see. The clouds in the sky hid the stars. Adam slowed the car and turned right.

I sat up, excited. "Are we there?"

He shook his head no, as the winding road continued to curve higher and higher. There were no street lights, no house lights, and no moon. Just blackness that threatened to swallow us. At the top of the mountain we turned left onto a gravel road and pulled down a dirt driveway. I saw my new home for the first time.

Adam had forgotten to leave any lights on. The lights from the car showed black windows that seemed unwelcoming and sinister. There was a strange lattice covering the windows that reminded me of prison bars.

Leaving the headlights on, Adam got out of the car and unlocked the front door. When we walked inside our shadows wobbled long and spooky across the floor. Adam clicked on the overhead light, and the dim light bulb barely ate up any of the darkness in the huge room. The bulb flickered then. I looked at it and shivered, wondering if the house was haunted.

The next morning, sunshine chased all the shadows back to the corners, and my spooky thoughts from the night before dissipated. What had appeared like a black cave when we first opened the front door turned out to be an enormous living room. The bedrooms were all upstairs, and the living room and kitchen were on the main floor. The house had stairs going down to the basement and more stairs going up to the attic.

My bedroom was right across the hall from my parents. It was thrilling to have a room close to theirs. I stood in the middle and spun with my arms open wide. It's a fresh start! They are giving me a new chance! I spied Kewpie in the corner and grabbed her for a dancing partner. With my arms clutched around her, I spun and dipped her. My room was as bright and shiny as a soap bubble, as sunlight flooded in through the two windows, splashing against the fresh, white painted walls. The light called to me, so I propped Kewpie against the wall--first straightening her dress-- and ran over to the wooden window sill to gaze out at the lodge pole pine trees. I never dreamed life could be this good.

We had only lived there for a few weeks, when I came home from school to Mama holding a box.

"You're moving down to the basement. Upstairs is our half, and the downstairs room is yours. Adam's been working on making a room for you for your birthday present." She followed me to my old room where I started to gather my things in the box. "No," Mama stopped me, "that box is for your books. You can keep three out, but the rest are going up to the attic. I'm sick of you reading all the time." She tapped a pack of cigarettes against her hand. "When I was your age I was always busy doing fun things. Of course, you're nothing like me. You're just like your Dad."

It was hard choosing my books. My preschool principal had told me years ago that books were her friends, and my books were friends too. I used them to help fill the hours I spent alone outside.

Finally, I picked out three and stuffed the rest of my belongings into a bag that I carried to my new room. As I passed Mama on the couch, she raised her hand to stop me.

"Remember, I don't want you upstairs unless you're eating or doing your chores."

I nodded, and left the room. There was a heavy, oak door at the top of the steps and Mama called to me, "Don't forget to close the door!"

Every step I took down to the basement was a twist in my gut.

The new room was a tiny bit bigger than my bed, with gray striped wallpaper on the walls that matched the blue-gray bedspread. At some point while I had been at school, Adam had built a desk in what once had been the tiny closet. I stared blankly at a nicotine yellow lamp hanging over the desk that cast an uncanny glow over my desk and walls.

There was a sliver of a window located a couple inches below the ceiling. I dragged my chair over to see if I could see out of it. But, I wasn't tall enough, and slumped down to the seat, discouraged. The window was level with the ground outside, and the glass was grimy with brown splotches from the rain splashing up the dirt. The constant dim light kept every color monotone; there were no sharp shadows or contrasts, only darkness smudging in to darker things.

A few days had passed when Mama walked in my room with another box.

"You can't keep your nice, new room clean. You're being disrespectful to what we've done for you. Pick a few of your favorites and pack the rest up. They're going to the attic."

I looked up at her from where I was sitting on the floor playing a board game by myself. My toys too? She tapped her foot and pointed to the box.

"You've got thirty seconds, or I'm doing it for you."

I packed up Peter, and my Barbies, and one of the dolls Mama made. I left the game and the other doll. She watched me rushing around and then peered under my bed to make sure I hadn't hidden anything.

Adam came downstairs to help Mama carry the box. She handed it to him, and then pointed her finger at me.

"I've booby-trapped the books, so I'll know if you sneak up there and get some. Can't out-smart me." Adam laughed at Mama's words as she turned to him with a smile. "She's sneaky, but I showed her." She looked back and continued, "Better keep your room clean, or I'll take the rest."

Mama left for the upstairs. I sat on my bed with my arms tight around me as my body shook. My chest felt tight, and I wanted to scream. I didn't pull my hair anymore when I was stressed. Instead, I bit my nails past the quick, something Mama slapped me for if she caught me. I chewed on my nails as the echo boomed inside of me.

It was about this time that Mama began calling me the fifth wheel of the family. She said to me in a matter-of-fact tone, "You know what a fifth wheel is? They're useless. They're not wanted. The other wheels are better off without it. Do you like being called Fifth wheel?"

I shook my head no. My nose was stuffy all of a sudden.

"I think you do. Otherwise you'd change. Now come here, Fifth Wheel, and clean the kitchen. You think you can do it right this time?"

I nodded and went over to fill the sink with soapy water.

Over the next few days, I worked hard at being good. She never saw me, I tiptoed into the kitchen to do my chores and shut the stairway door behind me when I was done. Things were going okay, until one night I hesitated in front of an open bag of cookies on my way down stairs. I reached in carefully, trying not to crinkle the paper, and slowly pulled one out. I looked at my prize with a smile and started for the door.

Mama was there, staring at me.

"What do you think you are doing?"

Cold chills ran down my back. I wanted to throw the cookie away from me and cover my face. She walked over and furiously whipped the package off of the counter.

"How dare you eat one of my cookies. You don't touch any food unless I give you permission."

I hid the cookie down by my side and mumbled, "I'm sorry Mama."

"I'll show you," she snapped. She stomped out of the room, returning with a laundry basket. Throwing the cupboards open, she swept cookies, chips, and other food off the shelves and into the basket. When it was full she lugged it to her bedroom.

My stepdad walked behind her shaking his head. He drove down to the hardware store and returned soon after with a new doorknob. There was metallic clicking while he installed the lock on their bedroom door. From that day on, she kept the food locked in her room, checking the door every time she left by rattling the doorknob.

"I've hidden the key. If you weren't such a sneak, I wouldn't have to do that. ." She shook her head as she walked away. "You really are a Fifth Wheel."

I was obsessed with guilt, and couldn't sleep that night. The next morning I went up to her, "Mama, I messed up. I'm so sorry. I'm turning over a new leaf! I'm going to do it right this time. Please give me another chance."

She responded with a bored sigh, "I've heard this so many times before. Your words don't have any meaning anymore."

There was nothing I could do. I went downstairs, seeing only failure in every part of my life. Every morning I was just going wake and do the whole nightmare all over again.

I didn't find any relief in school. Fifth grade was awful, and I wanted to quit. The boys pestered me and made fun of my name. I always hated my name, CeeCee, a blunt staccato that caused people to ask what it stood for, and didn't roll off the tongue in cute curls like Jennifer, or Elizabeth. Mama once told me that she couldn't think of one, so she picked it out of a celebrity magazine when I was a couple days old.

The kids also teased me about my hair, which was cut as high as my ears and uneven. Mama had told me, "Your hair looks ugly and stringy when it's long," and hacked my blonde hair even shorter with her scissors.

On picture day, I rolled my hair with a set of pink sponge curlers I had bought with my birthday money. I was hoping for a head of soft curls, like my old preschool principal. But instead, my hair curled into lumps. I can't do anything right! I viciously brushed my hair, before looking for my pink flower plastic barrettes and clipped them in. Better.

Mama laughed when she saw me at breakfast.

"Your hair looks ridiculous."

My hands flew to my hair, and I tried to pull the curls straight. I need water. She tapped the ash off of her cigarette into the ashtray on the coffee table, and said, "If you were a good girl, I'd fix your hair for you and make it look nice." She shrugged her shoulders and walked to the kitchen for a cup of coffee.

My clothing didn't help. Everything Mama had purchased for me was from her once a year trip to the Salvation Army, even though she didn't shop there for herself. Mama always said, "I would never waste money buying you nice things. You don't know how to take care of your stuff."

I struggled to keep my out-grown pants tugged down to cover my ankles. When I stood up in front of the class to read a book report, a boy from the back row called out, "Hey, where's the flood?"

My classmates all laughed, and the heat covered my face. I stuttered and lost my place on my paper. Sniffing, my finger ran down the paper trying to sort out the blurry words. My pants rose even higher when I sat down, so I pulled my feet cross legged in my chair.

That afternoon, I threw my books on the floor and flung myself on my bed and cried. Pounding came through the ceiling, Mama wanted me outside. I wiped the back of my hand over my eyes, and searched my drawers for an extra layer of socks, pants, and jacket. I pulled them on and ran out the door. The bitter cold of a Montana winter was still a shock to me after living in the desert.

Sometimes I'd unroll my plastic sled mat and slide down the driveway, just waiting until Mama would let me back in. On this day I was cold and lonely, so I dug myself a little fort in the snowbank left by the plow with my mittened hands. When it was big enough, I climbed and sat with my back against the icy wall. I closed my eyes. Laughing faces from the day flashed in my mind. No! No! No! Instead, I forced a daydream about being a famous singer, until my imagination went willingly, making me smile in the chilly shelter from the applause, and the flowers thrown at my feet. Outside, the wind howled and whipped the fallen snow. I stayed there until it was dusk, and I could come back inside.

The next afternoon it was below zero, and I shivered in my igloo. Pulling myself into a ball, I pressed my cold nose on my knees to warm it. Finally, I couldn't stand it anymore. My toes tingled when I climbed out, and tapped on the front door to ask Mama if I could come in.

"Thirty more minutes! The fresh air is good for you."

I didn't have a watch, so I went back to my snow fort to count the seconds.

The temperature was twenty-seven below zero when the television broadcasted weather alerts warning the public to stay inside because of the extreme cold. My neighbor drove by just as I climbed out of my snow fort. He rolled down his window and asked, his breath puffing in white clouds. "Hey! What are you doing out here?"

I didn't know how to answer him, so I shrugged and said, "Playing." I glanced up at the house and my stomach rolled when I saw Mama standing at the window, watching me.

When I came home from school the next day, Adam was waiting for me. He beckoned me over to the basement's woodstove. I could see my breath in the open room and was surprised to see there wasn't a fire going in the stove like there normally was.

"It's time you learn how to start the stove," he said.

Adam taught me how to twist the paper and load the wood stove with paper and kindling. My hands were black with ink by the time I finished the tight twists. He showed me how to keep an eye on the fire, and where the most seasoned part of the wood pile was to get wood. Every day I brought in armloads of wood, bits of bark sticking to my jacket. I watched the fire carefully to make sure the iron monster was fed to make the best heat.

I never turned on the electric heater in my room. Mama said that electric heat cost too much money, although she used it upstairs. There was a constant chill from the concrete that rose through the thin carpeting so I usually wore two pairs of socks. I had the fire roaring and held my hands before the flames for a few minutes to soak in the heat. Mama said the basement was part of her house too, so I had to go back to my room.

The next morning I woke up shivering. The fire had gone out in the middle of the night. Reaching down to the floor, I pulled my school clothes under the bed covers to warm them, and dressed under the blankets.

Mama stopped me on my way to the table with my cereal bowl.

"You didn't fill the woodstove very well last night. It went out. Did you sneak your heat on this morning? I'll know if you did."

I shook my head, no.

A few days later while I was doing homework, she tiptoed down the basement stairs and flung my bedroom door open with a bang. It scared me, and I jumped. She took my surprise as an admission of guilt.

"You sneaking your heater on, Fifth Wheel?" She bent down to touch the heater with her fingers to see if it felt warm.

My hand flew to my mouth to bite a nail, before I remembered. "No Mama. I know the rules."

I followed the rules, because the punishments were changing.

~ 13 ~
BIRTHDAY GIFTS

Mama called to me as soon as I walked through the door after school. Throwing my books on the floor, I ran upstairs. Mama was holding my stepdad's thick leather belt.

"I found a sock on your floor. I'm sick of telling you to keep your room clean. Go to your room."

I was shaking as I stumbled back down the stairs, my hand barely able to hold onto the railing. She walked down ten minutes later, each of her footsteps making me shake harder. With a sarcastic smile on her face, she tapped the belt against her hand, waving it in my direction to indicate she wanted me undressed. She brought down the belt, and her smile got bigger at the sound of the smacks. Ten times, twenty. When I couldn't stand the pain any longer I tried to crawl away, sobbing out, "Please Mama! Stop! I'm sorry!"

She laughed. "Where do you think you are going, little girl? Do we need to start this all over again?" She brought the belt down again, and it wrapped itself around my face. The belt fell again and again. I screamed until my throat burned. Finally, my bladder let go.

"Disgusting," she sneered, and left me huddled on the floor, still trying to shield my face. Her voice came down the stairs, "You better keep your room picked up. Or I'll be back."

Raised red welts covered my back and legs and a bruised triangle imprint of the belt swelled on my cheek.

The next morning I was stiff and sore as I rolled out of bed. I almost cried when I looked into the mirror, embarrassed to go to school with the mark on my face.

I walked into class with my cheek cupped in my hand, hoping to hide it. Mrs. Langley, my English teacher, asked me what happened.

"Oh my gosh," I cleared my throat and gave her my biggest cheesy grin, "I'm such a dork! Last night I slept walked, and fell into my dresser. That will teach me not to eat pizza before I go to sleep."

She smiled at me and said, "Pizza gives me bad dreams too."

The whippings came more frequently and were always for minor things. Eventually, when Mama told me to go downstairs she'd say, "Make sure you go pee first, you big baby!"

After the snow melted, Adam built me a playhouse made out of corrugated metal. It was sturdy enough to withstand the rain and the snow and became my sanctuary. I stayed inside listening to the rain drum on the metal roof and daydreamed that I belonged to another family. My pretend family had caring parents, a sister and two brothers who helped me do my chores. I'd sit still for hours in the playhouse with my eyes shut, while in my daydream my imaginary siblings and I climbed trees, played in grassy fields and picked apples. I rode pretend horses, ate imaginary meals, and never felt hungry. My imaginary parents hugged me often and told me I was a good girl. I'd sit in there smiling until my cheeks hurt.

On this day, when I finally opened my eyes I prayed, "Oh God, when I grow up, can I please have two little boys and two little girls? I would be so happy!"

I didn't want to leave my imaginary world, but when dusk came, I had to go inside. Dinner was a small plate of food at a table by myself, while I listened to my parents laugh and talk at a separate table in the other room. I tried to eat quietly so I could hear what they were saying; smiling when they said something funny as though they were sharing the joke with me.

When I got to my room that night I stood in front of the bathroom mirror and clapped my hands together as loud as I could. I know I can get used to this! I had recently begun flinching at loud noises that the boys made at school, especially when they made abrupt movements with their hands. Some of the boys had noticed my nervous response and worked to get a reaction out of me. Every time I reacted, I yelled at myself. Stop doing that! You're making it worse!

I carried a pink spiral binder to every class, filling the pages with random thoughts and drawings. I thought about death a lot, not so much my own, but of famous people, soldiers, and the Holocaust. I wondered if there was peace for them after they died.

One day, we skipped our math class and watched a movie on the Heimlich maneuver. I doodled in my notebook and looked up when everyone laughed at the dramatic choking man.

The next day the teacher sat on a stool in the front of the room, and read Tom Sawyer. I played with a round piece of laminated cardboard that came from the end of my pencil sharpener. I was trying to hold it against my lips with suction, and in the next second it was pulled down my throat. I reached in to grab it, but only pushed the slippery circle further down with my fingers. My heart beat fast as I sat there for a moment, not knowing what to do.

Slowly, I stood up from my desk. Mrs. Langley had been looking through the bottom of her glasses at the book, and lifted her head to examine me. Her eyes appeared large through the lens. She put the book down.

"CeeCee! What are you doing? CeeCee?? Sit down! Oh my gosh! Someone get the nurse!"

With my brain buzzing and dark, I staggered up to the teacher. She jumped up from her stool and laid her hand on my back. The pain of not being able to breathe was fading as she reached around me to do the Heimlich-Maneuver. My body crumpled forward in slow motion. She tried to hold me up at the same time as she drove her fists into my diaphragm. My vision grayed and then tunneled into black stars. All the echoes melted away.

It was peaceful, the first embrace of peace I had in a long time. I surrendered to its arms.

Whoosh! The cardboard shot out of me and air rushed in. I burst into tears, and Mrs. Langley hung on to my arm for support as she shook like a leaf. It was four days before my eleventh birthday. I knew God had spared me. Up until movie day, Mrs. Langley had not known the Heimlich maneuver. That night, after I crawled into bed, I whispered to God, "Thank you for my birthday present," and blew him a kiss.

I was a celebrity at the school over the next few days. The girls were nicer and came up to tell me that they were sorry if they had ever been mean to me.

The boys elbowed each other, "Did you see how purple her face was? That thing flew way over here and almost hit me!" I made them tell the story again and again to keep it fresh in their minds.

When Mama found out she was embarrassed. "How could you have been so stupid? Do I need to slap your face again like I did when you were little, because you can't keep crap out of your mouth?"

"No, Mama. I learned my lesson."

She rolled her eyes and found a note card in her desk to thank my teacher.

From then on when I came home from school I had to go upstairs and tell Mama if I behaved myself during the day. She warned me, "You know, I am in constant contact with your teachers. They tell me things." I never knew what my teachers said.

Mama would then go over the list of rules I had broken during the day. On this day she said, "Well, Fifth Wheel, you had too many clothes in the laundry." I eased my weight from one foot to the other as I waited for her to finish the lecture and dole out the discipline. It could be one of many things; take my meals away, extra chores, or the belt. "I want you to clean my bathroom to help you remember to only put two pants in the laundry." The punishment was light this time, and I held in my sigh of relief.

There was no time to go outside today. After I cleaned her bathroom it was time for dinner, and then kitchen chores.

After dinner Mama allowed a half hour of television time to watch The Cosby Show. My spot in the living room was on a bench near the kitchen. I told myself, Mama and Adam love you, they want you here, and tried to scrounge up the same cozy feelings that my day-dreamed family gave me. The daughter on the T.V. show said something cute, and the dad praised her. I hoped Mama didn't see, but she did. From the other side of the living room she snorted.

"Too bad you aren't more like her."

I stared at the T.V. antennae trying to swallow, while the laugh track went on in the background.

After the show, I grabbed my pajamas and tiptoed up the stairs for the upstairs bathroom. It was Wednesday, the night I could take a bath. As I walked past Mama on the couch, she arched an eyebrow at me.

"Remember, I'm listening."

I nodded and closed the bathroom door behind me. I stared at the door knob for a moment, wishing I was permitted to lock it, and then turned on the water for the bath. My heartbeat increased as the water rose, and when it reached three inches I wondered if I dared add any more. Loud slaps against the door made me jump.

Mama threatened through the door. "I'm coming in there to measure that water."

I hurried to turn the water off and huddled under my towel, praying that she didn't burst in with a belt. After a few minutes, when I didn't hear anything more, I climbed into the water to take my bath.

I hated bath day.

Two days later, Mama walked into the kitchen while I made a sandwich at the counter. She regarded my hair with sharp scrutiny.

"Don't you care how you look? Your hair is greasy, you look like a slob."

I blinked, there was no safe answer.

She tapped her fingers nails on the counter. "Did you finish your homework?"

Holding the peanut buttered knife in the air, I wondered; what homework do I have left? She slapped my face with the back of her hand.

"Don't roll your eyes at me."

My nose burned like fire, the pain made me feel like I smelled pepper.

"Sorry Mama," I said and tried to subtly turn my back towards her to finish my sandwich.

My grandparents were due for a visit that month. My grandfather was charmed by the little playhouse. "CeeCee, show me your new house."

We walked inside, and he sat in the red chair.

"It's nice." His eyes glittered as he looked at me. "You're my favorite grandkid. Let's play a game."

I tried to avoid the clubhouse every time he visited, but it didn't matter. He always found me.

Adam's mom and dad, aunt and uncle also planned to visit that summer. I was excited to see them and counted down the days on a pocket calendar for when they were to arrive. Whenever we had company, there was more food available, and Mama didn't watch for ways to punish me because the guests took her attention.

They arrived in a huge bustle of activity. The luggage was piled into the front room, while everyone interrupted one another with details of their trip. My step-grandparents slept in my happy bedroom upstairs, while my stepdad's old aunt and uncle squished together on my twin bed in the basement.

Adam took them all downstairs and showed them the book shelf and desk he had made. They complimented him on doing a good job, and he beamed with pride. My step-grandma turned to me and asked, "So how do you like school, CeeCee?"

I smiled. "Oh I love it. I'm getting good grades in all my classes." Mama arched her eyebrow at me. I excused myself and ran outside.

The next day, my step-grandma said at breakfast, "Come with me to the drug store. You do have one around here, don't you?"

I laughed and answered, "Yep, right in town."

"Oh good, I want to get you a little something since you just had your birthday. Does that sound like fun?"

We drove to the drugstore, and she huffed a little when she pulled her stout body out of the car. "Wooowee, the elevation here is taking its toll."

I nodded, even though I didn't know what she meant. She took my hand and led me into the store.

"Go ahead and look," she said, "Find something you want."

I skipped up and down the aisles with excitement. Anything I wanted! After scanning the toy aisle I pointed to some wash-off nail polish.

"This right here?" She grabbed it off the shelf, and I nodded with a big smile. "Oh, this is cute," she smiled back at me and put it in her cart.

When we returned home, Mama demanded I show her what was in the bag. She pulled out the pink bottle and sighed.

"What a sneaky little girl CeeCee is. She knows she isn't allowed to wear nail polish."

My step-grandma wrinkled her brow and said, "Oh, but this kind washes off with water."

Mama shook her head. "Not even the play kind. She'll just make a mess."

"I'm sorry, I didn't know." My step-grandma's eyes flitted towards me, and then cut away. She was someone else who now saw me as a bad girl.

I tried to say that I was sorry too, but it didn't matter. The family stayed for two more weeks and I was scared for them to leave. Mama would hit me once they were gone. Mama was angry with me, and there was no escape from her anger.

~ 14 ~
SIXTH GRADE

Next to our house was a neighbor's corral that ran along the property line. The fenced area was occupied by a single horse. I suppose once he was pure white, but his coat looked gray because the corral was thick with mud. He watched for me over the top of the splintered wooden rail with his ears pointed and flared his nostrils whenever he saw that I had noticed him.

One afternoon I brought my old hair brush with me and climbed up the fence to sit. Carefully, I situated myself to avoid the roughest parts of the rail. He whinnied and ambled over.

"Good boy, nice pony." I put my arm around his neck, chuckling when he nuzzled the top of my head. He blinked his dark eyes with long white eyelashes, and his muzzle prickled my hand when he searched for an apple core that I sometimes saved for him. As I patted his back the dust flew up in clouds. I swept down his sides with the old brush, trying to clean the dirt off. He didn't move when I stretched from the top rail to reach what I could on his other side. When I stopped to clean out the brush he nudged me with his nose. The loose hair floated up and away in a thick, gray cloud.

"You're a good boy," I murmured and leaned across his broad back to give him a hug.

I always wondered what it would be like to ride him, but was too nervous to try it. I heard that horses bucked if they didn't want a rider. I wouldn't want to force him to do something he didn't want to do.

Mama felt sorry for the horse. "Haven't you fed that poor animal yet?" "Why are you reading when that poor horse needs grass?" "Why didn't you brush him?" "Why are you reading a book when he's suffering?" She'd shake her head in disgust. "So cruel. If I were your age I'd never pick you for a friend."

I never knew how to answer the questions, so I'd nod. I'd take the black-handled scissors out to our field and cut laundry baskets full of grass. I cut grass until my hands became red with blisters. Mama had said that one basket was not enough.

A few weeks later, I was building a miniature village out of rocks behind the playhouse.

"Hey there!" a man's voice rang out. I looked up and saw a man leading the white horse by a rope up the road. "Found this horse running loose down our street. Have any idea where he belongs?" Excited to help, I jumped up to point out my neighbor's house.

Mama stood at the living room window watching me. She wrenched open the screen door and in a low growl said, "Come here."

I looked over at her with shock. I thought Mama would be happy that I had helped the man. Her hands shook with anger.

"That horse finally escaped, and you made him go back to the filthy living conditions he lives in. It's your fault he has to live that way. You've ruined his life." I lowered my head as she ranted, "You are such an uncaring, unloving person. You disgust me." After she slammed the door closed I ran back to my rock village, my lip trembling as I edged the miniature street with pebbles and flowers.

I was eleven years old when my body started to develop some womanly curves. Mama brought me to the doctor because she thought that there something was wrong with me. The doctor explained to the both of us that I was starting puberty. Mama cut my food portions even smaller, and my curves melted back into my bony frame.

When Grandpa came to visit, he was delighted with the changes he saw in me. "Come see Grandpa," he said when I resisted. Mama continued to round up all the adults and leave for the day, abandoning me with him.

Mama still bought my food separate from theirs, the same generic items every week, even though they didn't eat it themselves. "You can't have adult food," Mama explained. My days were filled looking for things to eat outside. Dandelion leaves were not my favorite, but they grew everywhere. I nibbled the jagged edges of the leaf, avoiding the veins- they were too bitter. Once I tried a dandelion flower because it smelled so sweet, but spit it out with disappointment. The yellow flower was dry and bitter and the petals choked me. I did like long grass though, and pulled apart the grass shoots to eat the tender, light green ends. I piled my lap with purple clover flower heads like a feast and plucked the petals off to bite the tiny bit of honey in the white ends of the petal tips.

Autumn was my favorite season. Dried rose hips were everywhere, and they were like seedy raisins. I picked the tiny red Kinnikinnick berries that hid in the low shrubs, celebrating if I had a small handful. They were fun to eat, the outsides crunched, but the inside had a melting, powdery-white center. I pulled apart pine cones looking for the seed pieces, bit along the lengths of pine needles for their tang, and nibbled on flower stems. I tried the gooey sap that hardened in spots on the tree bark, but it was gross and stuck to my teeth.

People at school asked me, "Why are you so thin?"

"I'm not skinny. I just play outside a lot."

One afternoon, I came home from school and found Mama lying on the couch. She was softly moaning, so I ran over to check on her and discovered that she was really sick.

"Mama, do you want something?"

She lit a cigarette with shaky hands and answered sarcastically, "You're just like my sister, such a selfish, sneaky liar." She moaned and cuddled her heating pad, then took another drag off her cigarette. She blew out the smoke and said, "You know, your aunt used to torture me when I was little by pinning my legs over my head and holding them there knowing I couldn't breathe. You act just like her, always arguing and rolling your eyes."

She watched the smoke swirl against the ceiling a second before stabbing the cigarette toward me. "And I know that you're still sneaking food. Don't deny it."

I opened my mouth, but she silenced it with a look. "I know. You'll try to be better. I'm sick of that promise. Don't try to be better. Just be better."

She shook her head. "Just like your Dad. Every time I look at you it's like he's staring back at me. I remember what a disgusting waste of space he was. If I'd known what you'd be like, I would have never had you. Maybe then Adam would want kids. Oh, I know you're jealous of him. Did you know after the first year with you, he wouldn't even talk about another kid?"

My mouth fell open, and I backed away, destroyed by her words. The terrible ache almost drove me to my knees.

Mama stayed on the couch every day, wrapped up in a striped afghan. Those first few days I made an effort to care for her, but she told me to keep away. She had my stepdad to take care of her by helping her bathe and bringing medicine. Mama became more withdrawn when she learned that the only cure was surgery.

"You're going to be ok, Mama." I said, bringing her a cup of tea.

"You're going to regret how you treated me, CeeCee."

"I'm sorry Mama. I will try to be better."

"It's too late for that. Go away."

Mama said she might die during the operation. I shivered with the thought on my way to my room. My stepdad didn't want me, and I would be forced to live with my real Dad. He was scary, mostly because of all the horrible things Mama had said about him.

Mama stayed locked in her room. Adam shrouded her in a long jacket and a blanket when she left for the hospital, leaving me at home. I didn't go with my stepdad when he visited Mama in the hospital. She told me I would make it worse.

I went to bed crying every night, because Mama didn't want to see me. Still, life was easier when she was gone.

My stepdad always followed Mama's rules. He didn't talk to me very much when Mama was around, or interfere with her punishments.

But while Mama was in the hospital, Adam and I talked a little bit. He didn't monitor what I ate, and didn't enforce the rule about staying outside. I came and went through the front door, washed my clothes and had a bath when I wanted to. The freedom was bliss, and I thought he was wonderful.

Mama stayed in the hospital for several weeks. When she returned home, she shuffled from room to room in a thin pink house coat with her hair limp and tangled down her back. Grandma came up to help take care of Mama during her recovery. Mama wouldn't talk to her, because she caught Grandma drinking one morning, even though Grandma had promised she wouldn't.

A few days after Mama was back, I came home from school to find a sandwich sitting on the counter.

Mama waved her skinny hand towards it. "Eat it. I made it for you."

I moved slowly towards it, my brain trying to understand that she had made it for me. I picked it up; the bread was as stiff as cardboard. Still stumbling through my thoughts, I said, "Mama, the bread is stale..."

WHACK! She cracked me with the back of her hand across my face. I fell against the counter. She hissed, "YOU ungrateful jerk. I made you that sandwich. You eat it."

Standing up, I forced it into my mouth with my lips quivering and a lump in my throat. Grandma's glazed eyes found me, and she slurred alcohol fumes in my face.

"Ohhhhhh CeeCee, she's hurting and still made you ssandwich."

Mama pulled her bathrobe tight, and shuffled into her room. I didn't see her again for a few days.

As her health returned, Mama and Adam picked up their old routine of shopping every Saturday. I was the Fifth Wheel of the family and not included. They never told me where they were going, or when they would return. If I asked Mama, she'd laugh, "Why do you want to know? Thinking of sneaking back inside?"

Before they left, Mama unplugged the beige curly telephone cord from the receiver and took it with her. At the door she turned back and said, "You know, we like to drive around the corner and watch you. We see if you sneak back inside after we leave. We'll catch you one day."

I swallowed and nodded. I was afraid to use the bathroom in case they returned while I was in the house. I didn't want to get the belt.

Mama had come up with a new way to hit me with the belt. Just before my twelfth birthday, she called me to the table and sat across from me, her hands folded in front of her like we were at a business meeting. In a calm voice she said, "I have decided that each offense you commit will be worth twenty belts. I'll divide the amount by four and you'll receive them throughout the day." Her face was stony when she rose from the table and walked to the living room. I went downstairs to my room feeling numb.

From then on if I broke one of her rules, I had to stop what I was doing throughout the day and come inside for the belt. Mama didn't punish me that way for long, though. It didn't satisfy her, because by five whips I wasn't screaming yet.

Her suspicion and paranoia grew in other ways. During my long walks through the mountain roads I'd met a girl named Sandy. One day, Mama asked me where I had been, and I blurted out my friend's name.

"I don't trust you," she said, and went to the phone. I waited outside and listened through the open window as she adamantly talked to Sandy's mom.

"You know how kids are. Mine just hates to be outside. Don't let her in." Mama let out a light laugh at Sandy's mom's response. "Oh I know! By the way, don't feed her either. She won't eat dinner if she has snacks. I don't do all that cooking for nothing, right?" There was more laughter, and then Mama hung up the phone. She came to the door with a tight smile. "I took care of that problem. Sandy's mom will be letting me know if you sneak into her house."

I went over there a few days later, biting my nail as I rang the doorbell to see if Sandy was free. The door opened, and Sandy's mom stood in the dark doorway looking at me. I opened my mouth to ask if Sandy could come out, when she thrust her arms and gathered me into a big bear hug.

"You come right in here, I will never ever tell!"

From that day on Sandy's mom took me under her wing. She fed me sandwiches, potato chips, and cookies. Once, she gave me a big glass of Kool-Aid. I was horrified when I saw my lips stained cherry red and started crying, "My mom will kill me!" She ran and got a wash cloth so that I could scrub off the dye.

Another afternoon, after I returned from Sandy's house, Mama called me inside. "I drove down there to see if you were sneaking into her house."

I nearly keeled over as the blood drained from my upper half of my body. She examined me for a minute. "Don't you forget, I'm always watching."

Sandy's mom and siblings kept an eye out for Mama whenever I was at their house. There were a few times I had to dive out their back door, because they said she had driven by.

In the meantime, my front teeth were coming in crooked. So, for my twelfth birthday, Mama took me to an orthodontist to be fitted for braces.

"This is your birthday present," she said, as she opened the office door. In the waiting room she muttered, "Although we wouldn't need to be doing this if you hadn't sucked your thumb."

The orthodontist did several x-rays and a plaster mold of my teeth. He beckoned Mama and Adam to come to the dentist chair where I sat with the paper bib clipped around my neck. Knotting his eyebrows together, he tapped his chart.

"There seems to be something going on with her jaw. It's just not lining up right. I'm thinking it's going to take surgery and head gear to correct the problem."

Mama opened her eyes wide. "Oh, wow. That's not good. Thank you for telling us."

We never went back to the orthodontist. Mama explained that it was because of her surgery costs. I was relieved because I didn't want head gear. As the years went by, she didn't take me to another dentist until we'd moved out of state.

Now that I was twelve my next door neighbor asked me to babysit. I loved babysitting, and it became regular employment. I always went over a few minutes early, hoping my presence would encourage the parents to leave as soon as possible. I'd flip on Sesame Street and sit down to watch it with the kids. Oscar still made me smile.

A few minutes after the parents shut the door, I'd peek out the window to make sure they were gone, then run to the kitchen. I'd search the cupboards, reaching my hands far back for some forgotten food that I could eat unnoticed. I ate waxy pink chocolate chips, raw spaghetti noodles, and children's vitamins. I ate the olives out of the lunch meat. I ate spoonfuls of peanut butter, cheese, and handfuls of cereal. When I was done I'd smooth the food so that it still appeared full and pray that the parents wouldn't notice and tell Mama.

The children's mom started having me come over, even when she was home. She usually would ask just before I left for the night, "Do you mind watching the kids tomorrow while I do the dishes? I'll pay you a dollar and some lunch."

I always jumped at the opportunity.

One time, as she handed me a soda for my lunch, she said, "Don't take this the wrong way hun, but I don't like your mom. Any time you need a break, you come over here."

I was taken aback by her words and only nodded.

I used my babysitting money to buy Mama presents to show her that I loved her. I craved those few seconds when her face softened, and she thanked me. Once, I ordered a flower arrangement. Another time, I found a lost kitten and presented it to her. I knew her love for animals might spill over to me when she cradled it and stroked its fur. The whole thing almost fell apart when the kitten's owner showed up, but he let us keep it.

Then one day, the presents stopped working. Now, when I brought her a prize she said, "If you really loved me you would obey me."

I'd always promise her, "I'll turn over a new leaf Mama," and hoped that she would give me another chance.

She answered the same way every time, "I've heard that before. You sound like a broken record," before turning away from me.

~ 15 ~
SUMMER AND DAD

Sixth grade ended and all my school books were stored away. I sat on the front step scratching a bug bite on my leg while I watched a hummingbird dip its beak into a columbine. Mama made me jump when she appeared at the door. She told me to pack my bags, because she was sending me down to Arizona to stay with my maternal grandparents for a couple weeks. I was twelve, and I will never forget that summer.

Grandpa started in right away after I arrived at their house. Every day, he made me come out with him to his dusty shed, I'd tell myself, "He says he loves me. He loves me. He loves me." He sat on an old milking stool and rambled about his fantasies before he molested me. The stories were scary, involving some of his favorite thirteen year-old prostitutes in Mexico. I stared at the closed shed door with a sick heart, imagining ways I could bust it down to get away.

The abuse had been going on for six years now. He knew how to compel and bully me into making me do what he wanted. "This is our special secret," he warned, before putting his finger over his lips. "Don't you tell anyone. You want to be a good girl, don't you? You could get ol' Grandpa arrested. Besides, it would kill your Grandma."

About a week into the visit, I hurried out of the shed and up to the back door, crunching over the red lava rocks that Grandma had in place of grass. I felt dirty and scrubbed my hands against the sides of my pants. I didn't know what I could do to ever feel clean again.

The back door was wreathed in morning glory flowers, the vine holding its weight with the tiniest of green tendrils woven in the cracks of the door frame. Before walking inside, I touched the centers of a few of the flowers, dotting each of my fingertips with yellow pollen. The flowers reminded me of my childhood fairy book, on a picture page that said, "This is a safe, happy home." With frustrated tears in my eyes, I brushed the pollen off my hands and went inside.

A few hours later, Grandma snuck into my bedroom where I had been hiding with my book. She clutched two brown alcohol bottles, one of them pinned under her arm. With exaggerated tip-toe steps, she went to my dresser to pull out a drawer, and hid her bottles among my clothing. She winked one mascaraed eye at me and whispered, "It's our little secret," before tip-toeing back out the door. I returned to my book and didn't come out of my room until dinner.

I heard Grandpa drive his Lincoln up the driveway, returning from a run to a chain restaurant. He came inside with a slam of the door that I imagined sent the morning glory flowers rocking.

"Dinner!" he called.

I put down my book and ran out to the kitchen. The scent hit me before I turned the corner, mmmm, fried chicken. The jaunty red and white chicken bucket that sat in the center of the tablecloth seemed bottomless as Grandma pulled more and more food out of it. There were biscuits, coleslaw, corn on the cob, and chicken. My eyes grew bigger with each food discovery as I rubbed my hands together and called for the drumstick. We were like a family right out of a commercial on the television.

After dinner was cleaned up, Grandma disappeared into her room for a while. An hour passed before I saw her again with her hands flapping out to the side as she wobbled for balance just before she stumbled into the hallway wall. My heart leapt to my throat until I realized that she was drunk.

She swung her head like it was very heavy and blinked her eyes trying to focus, her hair puffing out hair like dandelion fuzz. She looked over at me with glazed eyes. Her pupils sharpened and her eyes turned mean. Icy chills ran down my back. I had never seen Grandma with mean eyes before. With leaden steps, she stumbled over to the coffee table and snatched up a hair ribbon. She whipped it in my direction and slurred.

"You are a horrible daughter to my precious girl! How could you treat her that way? She tells me the things you do! Horrible! Horrible Girl!"

I flinched, even though the ribbon whips didn't hurt. Backing away, I ran outside hoping to find Grandpa to rescue me.

The driveway was empty; he had already driven away in the Lincoln. My shadow stretched out before me in the last pink rays of sunshine as it set behind the desert horizon. The echo in my heart boomed as I scanned for someplace to hide. There was nothing around but sand, cactus, and the detestable shed. My head hung low when I walked back inside.

Grandma was still screaming in the living room, oblivious that I had ever left. All I could do was to cower down and repeat, "I'm sorry Grandma. I will try. I will try to be a better daughter."

I never saw Grandpa come home that night. Grandma finally collapsed on the couch, exhausted from her tirade. Her mouth drooped opened, and she was soon snoring with a nasal, buzzing sound. I walked to my bedroom and pulled open my clothing drawer to get out my pajamas. The clinking sound of the bottles rolling inside made my stomach sink. What if Grandma finds them tomorrow night? Will the alcohol make her yell at me all over again? I wanted to run away, but where could I go? I spun in a circle, half hoping to find a hidden wardrobe that might take me to a new land. My eyes fixed on the mirror on the opposite wall, suddenly noticing that the metal scrolling around the mirror looked like it had black curlicue demon eyes. Climbing back in bed, I lay my head on my pillow and tried not to imagine it staring at me as I struggled to fall asleep.

When the summer was over I packed my brown suitcase and returned back home. Mama asked me if I had been a good girl. Nausea rolled right up the back of my tongue when I answered with my happy-mask on, "Yes, I had a great time Mama. Thank you for letting me visit them."

On the inside I was screaming, please please make this stop!

Finally, I pushed it down.

Seventh grade would be starting in a week. I threw myself into creating a whole new look. Junior High was really moving up in the world. I promised myself, "No more shaking and flinching around boys! No choking or doing anything weird."

I asked Mama if I could use some of my saved money to buy myself a few things for the year.

"Salvation Army's not good enough for you?" she asked.

"I just want a few extra things." I held my breath as I waited for her to answer. She called to Adam to take me with him the next time he left for town.

A few days later he dropped me off at the mall. "I'm headed to the Auto Parts store. You have an hour." He tapped his watch to show me he was serious and drove off.

It was my first time in the mall. I pulled the heavy door open and walked into a bright arboretum that had a tree growing in the center. Circling it in orange squares were tables filled with people balancing plates of food. In the corner a blender buzzed at the Orange Julius stand.

The mall hummed with energy that danced through my body. Out of every store entrance there was an explosion of thumping music and signs on the window blasting BACK TO SCHOOL SALE! 50% OFF! My fists clenched tight with excitement around my babysitting money deep in my pockets.

I ducked into one store, and was immediately among all the other girls shopping with their friends or moms. They rifled through the clothes with high-pitched comments and quickly disregarded the clothes that weren't in style. Everywhere I turned, I bumped into someone. I felt like an idiot as I tried to get out of the way.

I grabbed a price tag on one of the shirts and pretended to look at it while I studied the store mannequin. A few minutes later, I left the store with a big smile, swinging a heavy bag that held two shirts that buttoned down the front and two pairs of pants.

With my remaining money I ducked into a hair salon for a real hair-cut. There wasn't a lot the hairdresser could do with my short hair. She clucked her tongue while she ran the comb through trying to part it on the left, then the right. She evened my hair out and showed me a new way to curl and style it.

The clock above the salon's mirror made me jump. I was late! I ran out of the salon and jogged through the mall clutching my bags, bottlenecked at one point by a family with kids and a baby stroller. When I reached the entrance Adam was already there sitting on a bench. He stood up, as I ran to him out of breath.

"I'm so sorry. I got lost. I didn't mean to make you wait."

He sighed, "Did you get what you need?" I nodded. He pushed the glass doors open, and we walked out to the car.

When we got home I asked Mama if I could show her what I bought. Her lip started curling as I pulled out my new shirt, and I immediately regretted sharing my clothes with her.

"That's what was so important to you?"

I just shrugged while I stuffed the clothes back in the bag.

The next day, the alarm clock went off before the sun rose. I waited at the bus stop with butterflies in my stomach, holding my new pencil box filled with the shiny goodies of a mini stapler, and compass.

My first day at the new school was amazing. There were a couple of girls in my Home Economics class that I clicked with right away. I stared at the ovens and bags of flour peeking out from the shelves above and couldn't wait to get to baking. When the teacher introduced herself she pulled out a pair of pajamas from a floral bag on her desk.

"This quarter, we're going to learn to sew! Pick your pajama pattern everyone!"

My face fell. I sewed enough at home fixing my clothing if anything ripped. Instead of sewing, I listened to my friend's conversations while poking holes in my instruction paper with the star shaped pattern marker. We whispered down the line of humming sewing machines any gossip we had picked up during the day. But my friends had the advantage over me in class. They could thread needles and cut fabric even while giggling and sharing stories.

The week the project was due I sewed like a freak. That Friday, the teacher clapped her hands, "Class! Time to wear them!"

I tried to pull the finished nightgown over my head; it became stuck. Stupid ears! I didn't need to hear my friend's howl of laughter to know that I looked ridiculous. Somehow, I had switched the neck and arm hole in my rush to be done. After thrashing for a few minutes, threads snapping, I finally tugged it over my head and stared pop-eyed at them.

"Shhhhh," I hissed, not wanting the teacher to notice the terrible job I had done.

She came by a few minutes later while we stood like soldiers at attention in our motley Home Ec uniforms. Shaking her head when she came to me, she marked down a "C" in her syllabus.

My friends giggled harder when I tried to wriggle back out. I was trapped in a tug-of-war when they tried to help me pull it off. The neck hole was too tight. Amy laughed while she cut me free.

During lunch time we claimed our table in the middle of the room. My friends shared their growing pains about their home life while they traded food. No one wanted my food because Mama made me use the same bags all week long, and they were covered with peanut butter and jelly. After a few minutes they slid over a couple cookies, or half a sandwich with a small comment that they were full.

While we talked I agreed with their family complaints just to have something to say. I learned all about them, but they knew very little about me. When they asked me even the simplest questions about my home life the words stuck in my throat. But even with the little that I shared, they still knew I had trouble with Mama.

One day at lunch, I threw a hard back book onto the table. There was a scramble between the two of them when they dove to be the first to pick it up.

"How did you get this?" Amy asked, holding the newest book in the series by Madeline L'Engle.

"The Librarian ordered it special, and held it for me," I said. They rolled their eyes; they knew the librarian had a soft spot for me.

Our school had an enormous library. The first time I had stepped inside the library, I just had to stand there a minute and breathe, with a smile growing on my face. All the books neat in their rows called to me. I drifted down each of the aisles, tapping my finger along the book spines, first pulling this one, then that one out to read the blurb on the back. I ended up checking out an armload and later piling them in my locker. I spent every study period seated at one of the long wooden tables devouring one after another, like a little kid at a dessert buffet.

The librarian saw how I loved to read and said, "Well, we must be kindred spirits. I love to read, too." She saw my pink spiral binder full of stories, "What's this?"

"Oh, stories. Poems. I've been writing them for a couple years."

"I'd love to read them," she said.

I felt instantly shy. No one read my stories. No one.

She smiled at me like she knew my thoughts. "No pressure," she said. "I know it's hard to share those private things."

I clicked open the binder and pulled out the first story. "It's ok, I don't mind. Here."

"I'll keep this in a special place until I'm through reading it," she said, patting the papers.

I swapped one story a week with her from then on. She always thanked me for sharing them and encouraged me to keep writing. She never thought my stories about death, or lost children were weird; instead, she said I had talent. She was my hero.

Not everything was wonderful during that school year. There was a boy in my History class named Billy, who made my school days miserable. We had to sit next to each other at the same long desk. Every day he made fun of me and called me names. He was one of the kids that hung around the popular kids, trying to impress them with coarse jokes, but never quite made it to the center of the clique.

One day he showed up with a new mechanical pencil. He made a big show of refilling his pencil with new lead. He glanced sidewise and saw me watching. He smirked as he centered the clear lead tube at the top of his desk. He clicked up the lead and then with a flash of his hand, jabbed me in the leg. I gasped and clutched my leg. I looked at him in shock.

The teacher raised his head and glared at me from his desk at the front of the room. He was a red faced burly man, with bushy eyebrows, bloodshot eyes, and a reputation for being mean. His voice boomed from his desk, "Are you having a problem, CeeCee? Do you need to leave?"

All the students looked up from their books, their heads swiveling my way. I swallowed and answered, "No, sir," before burying my face back in my book again.

Billy grinned again. He adjusted his glasses with his thumb and then clicked his pencil lead up, watching for my reaction. With a twisted smile, he thrust it into the top of my thigh. I flinched and bit off a yelp. Click! Click! Poke! Click! Click! Poke!

I moved my chair with a scraping noise to the far end of the desk. He followed until he was sitting right up next to me while I pressed against the table legs. A lump in my throat choked me, and my eyes began to burn. Don't you cry, don't you dare.

Over the tears, a thick red haze began to grow, strange and empowering. I felt its heat as I breathed out. "Stop it now!"

Billy continued his soft clicks on the pencil under the desk.

"Whatcha going to do about it?" He taunted and turned a page in his work book.

I copied his pretense of reading, "If you don't stop, I'm going to poke you back!"

With that threat, I raised my wooden yellow pencil. His lips curled in a sneer. I looked over and saw the lead was broken, hanging sidewise off the tip of the pencil like a tongue. He flicked the lead off with his finger. My hands were shaking when I grabbed the plastic pencil sharpener that sat on the desk and twisted in the pencil. I blew off the imaginary shavings and looked square into his eyes.

"I mean it," I warned.

Staring back, he clicked his pencil one more time as a challenge. I thought I was bluffing, but when he made a sudden move towards my leg, I stabbed his arm. In horror, I jerked the pencil away. Billy squealed when he saw a piece of lead still in his arm.

The history teacher threw back his chair and stormed over to my desk. He loomed over me, the veins in his forehead bulging. He looked from Billy to my still upraised pencil in my frozen hand. Spit sprayed from his mouth. "What..? Get out of my class! Don't ever let me see you again!"

I waited outside the principal's office hunched in a chair. When she called me in her face was firm, so I started talking before I even sat down in the plastic chair.

"I was defending myself," I said. Her glasses reflected the overhead light, and I couldn't see her eyes to know if she believed me.

When I finished she indicated her finger to tell me to come near. "Let me see those poke marks."

I blushed to my hair line as I tugged down my pants, and stood in my underwear while she leaned forward to examine my leg. She sat back in her swivel chair and cleared her throat.

"Hmmmm. Go on and wait in the hallway until the bell rings for your next class. I'll address this with you later." With a dismissive wave, she sent me from her office.

My stomach knotted on top of itself during the rest of my classes. Several kids came up to let me know that Billy had left for the doctors. "Your mom is going to have to pay his bills!"

When the final bell rang for the day, I sat frozen in my chair. I didn't want to go home. Finally, I got my legs moving to the parking lot, but I couldn't board the bus. Instead, I walked back and forth on the sidewalk past the opened door. The bus driver let off the air brakes as a warning for me to board. My legs were shaking when I climbed up the steps. Grabbing the seat in front of me to stop my shaking, I rested my head on my arms. When Mama found out she was going to hurt me. Would she stop at twenty for something as bad as this? Would she stop at thirty?

I was nauseous when I got off the bus and slowly walked up our dirt road. Quietly, I opened and shut the back door and ran to my room. There was no place to hide in the little room. I curled up in a fetal position on the bedroom floor with my hands clasped together behind my neck. Tears ran down my face, soaking the thin carpet. Horrible images began to flash through my mind of the pain that was about to come. I begged God to save me. I had no words to pray, it came out as, "Please, please, please, Jesus!"

Inside of me a small voice questioned, what's God going do? He's invisible. How can he prevent my parents from coming down the stairs? They'd walk right through him. But I couldn't stop praying.

The sound of the phone ringing carried down the stairs, two rings, three rings. Then the heavy thuds of my stepdad's footsteps overhead as he made his way to answer it. It was the boy's parents. A thin whimper escaped my mouth, my heartbeat pounding in my ears.

I heard Adam say, "She did? Oh really," before his voice broke down into a series of low rumbles. I shook even harder, my teeth rattling in my head, "Please, please, please, please."

Out of nowhere, a strange heat rolled over me. I'd never felt anything like it before. The heat enveloped me in a heavy peace that destroyed my fear. Instantly, I stopped shuddering and slowly uncurled my body to stretch flat on the floor. I didn't notice the cold rising from the cement floor. Instead, I felt warm and calm. In the deepest part of me, I knew that I was going to be okay.

It was the first time I ever remembered taking a breath without fear.

My stepdad's deep voice carried down the stairs, but I couldn't understand what he was saying. The phone slammed into its receiver and then pounding footsteps across the ceiling as Adam found Mama.

And then, nothing.

I lay there in the peace and waited, and waited, until I lost track of time. After a while I decided, I'm going wait in bed. I feel asleep right after I pulled the covers up.

My parents never came down the stairs that night. I never found out what happened during the phone call to this day.

It was a miracle.

The next day at school, I stood outside of History class and watched all of the other students file in. The teacher had told me not to return, so I didn't know what to do. I bit my nail ragged, and shrugged my book bag from one shoulder to the other. Finally, just as the bell rang I slid through the door.

The teacher scowled when he saw me and pointed his finger to a new seat across the room. Neither Billy nor the teacher made eye contact with me. I sat at my desk and tried to be unobtrusive, but inside I smiled.

By the end of the semester, I had a perfect grade in History. The teacher had to know that I was not a bad girl.

The day before classes were dismissed for the winter break, the teachers handed out awards of recognition. These awards were handed out in front of the parents and students in the school auditorium. I won one for a story I had written about the death of a young soldier. The Librarian gave a proud smile and tipped her head at me from her seat at the front of the audience. I blushed, my shoes feeling three sizes too big as I tried not to trip on my way up to the podium to accept it from the principal. There were random flashes of light that came from the audience as proud parents took pictures.

Mama gave me a tight smile when I sat back down. "You're smart just like your father."

During Christmas break, I flew back to Pennsylvania to visit my biological Dad. It was the first time that I had flown across the country by myself. I was on the verge of giddiness the entire way, my face pressed against the window admiring the silky blanket of golden clouds below us.

Over the intercom, the flight attendant announced that we would soon be arriving. I jumped out of my seat and ran down the aisle to the tiny airplane bathroom. Leaning over the little sink, I studied myself in the mirror. Will Dad recognize me? My heart fluttered in my chest at the reality of seeing Dad for the first time in five years. Will I recognize him? I tried to smile, and my reflection gave a horrific grin back; pale face and chapped lips. I licked my lips and smoothed my hair down with clammy hands, jumping when the pilot announced that everyone should return to their seats for the landing.

The airport terminal entrance was filled with people holding signs, and waving as we exited the plane. I searched the crowd for Dad in the sea of smiling faces. He stood to one side, his face expressionless, and held up one hand to acknowledge that he had seen me. I tried not to bump into anyone as I walked over. His face had new wrinkles, and he looked tired.

Dad grabbed me in a one-armed hug, while I gave him my best smile, my chapped lips splitting. We broke apart quickly, both of us looking in opposite directions as though we were complete strangers.

"H..hi Dad," I stuttered, feeling tongue tied. What could I say to Dad, when everything in my life was a secret?

"Hey, how are you doing, kiddo?" He answered. He seemed as uncomfortable as I was, as he grabbed my bag and strode out ahead of me to the airport doors.

We drove through the city and out into the country, the two of us sitting silent in his old truck. "Radio doesn't work," he said with a nod towards the instrument panel. He turned left by a silver grain tower and passed several green and yellow fields before he bumped down a grassy driveway hidden between the crops.

He lived in a farmhouse with eleven empty bedrooms. The house reminded me of a white chess piece sitting by itself on top of a checkerboard of the corn and wheat fields.

Dad opened the door with a huge rusty key and set my suitcase inside on the peeling kitchen linoleum floor. He cleared his throat and then said, "Here's home. I haven't been able to afford light bulbs for all the rooms, so there's only light in the kitchen, and in the living room." He handed me a silver flashlight to use to find my way to my bedroom and the bathroom.

I climbed the dark stairs, dragging my suitcase behind me with a scraping bump. Each time the flashlight flickered I froze and then gave the flashlight a ferocious whack. I threatened it, "Don't you dare go out!"

My bedroom had a lone window under an alcove that gave out a smidgeon of light. I smacked the flickering flash light, and the beam found a little cot with a green sleeping bag and a lumpy pillow. With slow steps, I walked over and picked up the pillow, giving it a sniff. It smelled like mildew, and I flung it back down. I moved to the bedroom window and pushed back the muslin curtain, trying to distract myself from the unpleasant smell and the strange room. It was a cloudy gray sky. Below my window I saw an old family grave yard with uncanny tilted weathered crosses. I groaned at the sight of the graveyard, and my room seemed even more cold and depressing.

The dark and the gloom carried over to the next day, which I spent huddled under a blanket on a broken-down brown couch watching T.V. While Dad was at work, I didn't use the bathroom. I didn't want to wander the spooky house by myself. I wasn't sure what I would meet in the shadows of long dark hallway, and the graveyard outside didn't help my imagination.

Dad and I didn't connect with each other the entire time I was there. Dinner was the two of us pushing food around on a plate with our forks and talking about the weather. At the airport terminal when it was time for me to board, Dad patted me on my head like I was a puppy.

Mama and Adam picked me up at the airport later that night. I went straight to bed when I got home. The next morning there was a box from Adam's parents sitting on the table for Christmas. They sent Mama and me sweaters as presents. Mine was a pale pink and made from real wool. Mama's was yellow. She frowned after she opened it and thrust it away from her.

"Ugh, Yellow just makes me look sick."

I pulled mine over my head, and laughed as the wool made my hair stand up all over with static. She looked at me.

"Pink looks so good on me. I wish I had gotten pink."

I tugged down the cuffs at my wrists. I loved the soft color so much.

"Do you want to trade?" I asked her.

Her smile was so big that I was happy to pull the sweater off and hand it to her.

"Here take it Mama! You're right, yellow looks much better on me."

Actually, yellow didn't look good on me either because my skin had the same olive tone as hers. She pulled the pink sweater on with a smile and turned away from me.

"Mama, that sure looks good on you."

She didn't answer because she was laughing at something my stepdad said.

She didn't talk to me again until after dinner. "Make sure you do a good job washing the dishes." I never wore the yellow sweater.

Christmas break ended and I went back to school. Mama was gone all day too, because she had begun working as a sixth grade teacher's aide at the elementary school. Every night, while I sat alone eating dinner, I listened to her in the other room tell Adam about how impressed she was with her wonderful kids.

After dinner was over and I was clearing the dishes, Mama pulled out the craft bin and hummed to herself while she assembled the next day's craft pieces. She loved doing crafts with the school kids. She told Adam, while cutting shapes out of the construction paper, "Oh one of the boys is so special, he's such a smart kid. And then there's this girl named Jessica, so sweet. She actually follows me wherever I go. She has the softest voice I've ever heard. Those kids really love me."

The little girl inside of me crumpled while I washed the dishes. I ran the water at a trickle so that I might hear if Mama said anything about me.

After I finished my chores, I walked into the living room and told Mama that I loved her. She paused with her scissors in the air, little scraps of colored paper scattered all around her. "If you were a good girl I'd do crafts, or make cookies with you too." I closed the stairway door behind me and trudged downstairs.

Despite my many sincere attempts to turn over a new leaf, Mama never did do crafts or bake with me.

Spring came with warm breezes that melted the snow after five frozen months. Spring was my favorite season. Sandy and I traipsed through the empty forest by her house, rediscovering our woods finally released from the thick winter snow. We found a cluster of little purple flowers that had pushed their way up through a patch of stubborn snowy remnants.

"You see that," I pointed to them in a poetic flush, "This is our special sign that hope always conquers."

We saw another colorful patch a little further away and ran over to investigate.

"Holy Buckets," Sandy said, gazing at the forest floor littered with torn envelopes, newspapers, and wet magazines half buried in pine needles. We grinned at each other over our incredible fortune and sifted through the paper mess looking for treasure. Sandy found a padded envelope that held a sample of knee high panty hose. I called dibs on it because it was my thirteenth birthday. She was not impressed with the knee highs, having already obtained permission to wear pantyhose, and tossed them over to me. "Happy birthday!" she shouted, and then threw handfuls of old letters in the air like confetti. She grabbed me by the hands and spun me around singing "It's your birthday! Cha! Cha! Cha!"

I ran home clutching my prize to my chest, and found Adam splitting firewood. He leaned against his axe like a cane, taking a break when he heard me call him. "Papa, guess what! There's some weird garbage in the woods up behind the hill."

His eyebrows went up, and he said, "What do you mean? Someone's been dumping garbage in our woods?"

I jumped up and down, my boots squelching in the mud, "Yeah! Yeah! And it's all over the place!"

After he finished his wood pile, he hiked up to the woods. When he came back, his face was red and his eyebrows furrowed deep over his glaring dark eyes. In all the years that I had I known him, I had never seen him so angry. He exploded, "Go!" and I ran for my room.

Ten minutes later, I heard the stairwell door slam open against the wall, and violent pounding down the stairs. I squeezed myself into the space between the end of the bed and the wall and tried to hide with my hands over my head. I had no idea why they were so angry, but it didn't matter if they were going to hurt me. I was astonished when they didn't burst into my room. Instead, my door shook as they both screamed that I was thief, a liar, and accused me of mail fraud. Mama shrieked, "You stole that mail! I know it! I'm calling the police on you right now! They're coming to get you, and they'll haul you off to jail!"

It got quiet for a minute, and then my door crashed open. I jerked in my hiding place. Mama thrust my birthday cake into my room with a fork stabbed into the top. She slammed it onto my desk and said, with a disgusted tone, "You eat your cake by yourself. Happy Birthday," and banged the door shut. They both pounded back up the stairs.

I was shaking when I crawled out from behind the bed, wondering what had happened, and if I was going to jail that night. I brushed my tears off with the back of my arm, trying to calm my hitching breaths.

My cake sat tilted on the desk, half on my math book. Picking up the fork, I put it into a corner of the pink frosted ballerina slipper that was surrounded by thirteen unlit pink candles. I tried to eat it. The cake tasted like sawdust, and my throat was choked closed from anxiety. Tears ran down my face as I pulled the knee high panty hose out of my pocket and tried it on.

The police never showed up, and neither Mama nor Adam brought up the stolen mail again. I never learned what happened with the police and the mail. I didn't even go back to the woods to see if the stolen mail was still there.

I was thankful they never brought it up again. Mama's discipline had gotten out of control. Just that week, she had accused me of rolling my eyes after she gave me a chore. Lightning fast, Mama grabbed a fistful of my hair and yanked me into the air. She dragged me across the floor, dangling from the hair she clenched. First she swung me over the back of the bench, and then she swung me like a bowling ball down the stairs. I pin-wheeled my arms wildly, and was saved from falling head first by a miraculous catch on the hand rail. It was the defining moment that I realized my mom could cause me serious harm in her anger. I didn't know what to do, or where to go for help.

I did know someone with a story that gave me an idea, though. There was a popular boy at our school who our teachers used to point out and tell us that he was a role-model for the rest of us students. He had given a presentation to the class about the many obstacles in his life that he had overcome through foster care and counseling.

The next day at class I gazed over the top of my text book at him with hope, maybe he could help me somehow. I was scared, but wrote a note in tiny words, "help me," and folded it into a tight, little square. When I went up to sharpen my pencil, I dropped the note on his desk undetected. The shaking started as I staggered back to my desk. I watched him unfold it and couldn't take a breath. My heart crashed against my ribs.

He turned to study the girl two seats across from him. With a sinking feeling, I watched as he got up and put his hand on her shoulder, leaning down to whisper in her ear that he would help her. She didn't deny writing the note, in fact she even nodded. Bile rolled up my throat when I saw her come up with a few tears. I realized that there was no help for me. I wasn't popular like the girl was, and didn't have the guts to tell him the note was from me.

My grandparents came for a quick visit over the weekend soon after my birthday. A few hours after they unpacked, Mama gathered up Adam and Grandma, and abandoned me again with Grandpa. She smiled at him and said, "You two enjoy your time." And leaned down to whisper in my ear, "Behave, don't give him any trouble."

Grandma gave me a cheery wave with her hand as she headed out the door, and called to us, "Have fun!"

Grandpa nodded at them, and answered, "Oh, don't worry about us." He turned to smile at me after the front door shut. The three of them were gone all day.

Not long after their visit I got into trouble again. Mama said she heard me sigh when talking to me so she sent me to my room without dinner. As I walked down the steps to my room the echo pounded inside of me.

I sat on my bed, and exhaled deeply as the red haze flared up inside the echo. I threw my pillow across the room and fumed when it tipped over the trash basket. Flipping off the light, I climbed under the covers and tried to sleep. My breathing began to hitch, ending with a low moan. I pulled the covers over my face. Something inside of me broke open with a scream. Life's so unfair! There's no escape! Hopeless tears poured out of me, in a room so dark I couldn't even tell my eyes were open. The more I cried, the more pain fought to be released. I suddenly didn't care what happened to me anymore. Hurt me, don't hurt me! I don't care!

The pain wrenched a high-pitched shriek from my core, "I hate you! I hate you! I hate you!"

I screamed and cried for over an hour. When Mama came downstairs, I expected a belt in her hands and didn't even care. Instead, she held a striped afghan. Mama held the afghan out to me and said, "I made this for you, CeeCee. Every stitch is an 'I love you.'" My tears shut off in that instant. I took it with shaking hands. "Oh, I am so sorry! I love you too! I love you Mama!" She smiled at me and left the room, while I wrapped myself up in the blanket of her love. So many stitches! Finally, finally, finally, I had the affection of Mama. I was overwhelmed with joy.

The next morning, I drifted over to where she stood drinking her coffee in the kitchen.

"Thank you again, Mama. I love my blanket."

She looked at me for a second as she set down the coffee cup. My heart fluttered, anticipating her smile. She gave a sarcastic laugh and rolled her eyes.

"Oh that. I only said that to get you to quit your screaming. I'm sure the neighbors could hear, how embarrassing! A big girl like you throwing a temper tantrum. You were ridiculous. I'd have said anything to get you to shut up."

My jaw dropped open for a second, before I grabbed my lunch. I ran out to catch the school bus. On the bus, I looked out the window to hide the falling tears, and grieved the loss of the meaning in the blanket's precious stitches.

~ 16 ~
THE DAY I BROKE

The temperatures soared the last few days of school. We sat at our desks waving notebooks to cool down, while we took our final tests. Then there was an energy burst to find and return all of our library books and clean out desks and lockers. When the final bell rang, we cheered and sent hundreds of balls of crumpled paper flying through the air before we ran out to the bus. Summer was here.

When I got home Mama was waiting for me with a suitcase. Just like the year before, she told me to pack my stuff because I was going to my grandparents.

My grandparents had moved to a new house, this one with a small yard. Grandma stayed in her room for most of the visit, either napping or reading. We didn't sing or make dinners together any more. In the mornings, Grandma left to run her errands or visited the hairdressers for the local gossip. She didn't invite me along; I was always left alone with Grandpa.

The instant Grandma pulled out of the driveway Grandpa would come find me and give the predatory nod towards the garage. I had barely developed in a feminine way at thirteen, starved skinny, but that didn't matter to him. I was powerless to escape him and felt strangled by hopelessness.

Then one day it ended.

The day began like any other. Grandma returned home from the hair dressers that afternoon with her hair teased into high curls. When her car door banged shut, I ran from Grandpa and hid in my bedroom. I sat trembling on the white chenille bedspread with my fist jammed against my mouth to keep from screaming. With deep breaths, I tried to slow my breathing. My eye caught the cracked leather bible on the night stand and I lunged for it. I flipped open the bible, whispering, "please, please," and stabbed my finger down on the page. Leaning close, I read where I had pointed.

The scripture was Matthew 5:27-30, "You have heard that it was said, 'You shall not commit adultery.' But I tell you that anyone who looks at a woman lustfully has already committed adultery with her in his heart. If your right eye causes you to stumble, gouge it out and throw it away. It is better for you to lose one part of your body than for your whole body to be thrown into hell. And if your right hand causes you to stumble, cut it off and throw it away. It is better for you to lose one part of your body than for your whole body to go into hell.' "

My hand grasped my throat in horror. God sees me as an adulterer. Fear shot through me in icy waves, and drove the air out of me. I thrust the bible away and stared blindly at the wall. The walls felt like they were closing in, every bit of oxygen sucked from the room. I gasped for air and prayed, "Oh God! Oh God! Oh God!" What have I done?

In a panic, I stumbled to Grandma's room. She had just arranged herself on the bed with her reading glasses on, one of her romance novels propped open on a little pillow on her lap. Startled, she looked up when I burst into her room. Gasping, with tears streaking down my face, I stuttered, "I've done something naughty with... with... with....," I couldn't say it.

"A boy?" she gently prompted.

"No!" My heart flew into my throat. I lied, "It was the man next door."

The poor old neighbor man didn't deserve to be accused. He was friendly. Every morning he talked to me in his calm, deep voice while he pruned his roses. He shared stories about his grandkids, and all his tricks for caring for his beautiful, red velvety roses. I had listened on the other side of the rose bush hedge, as the grass tickled my bare feet, and sipped from a glass of orange juice. Our talks were innocent, wrapped in the clean smell of morning dew and fresh cut flowers.

For a long time after that summer I couldn't stand the smell of roses.

Grandma remained very calm even as I continued to break before her. My face was running. I grabbed the corner of my shirt to wipe my eyes and nose. She spoke to soothe me with gentle words that I never really heard. She repeated, "Everything's okay, everything's fine." When I stopped crying, she sent me back to my room to rest. I sat on the edge of the bed staring at the mirror with the scroll-worked demon eyes. It was over for me now. I could not fix this.

That afternoon, Grandpa came to my bedroom, and told me to get up.

"You're coming with me while I run to the store." Grandma looked over the top of her book as I passed her door.

I walked out to the car like a zombie, barely having sensation in my numb hands to find the door handle to open the car door. We drove for a few minutes without talking. I stared out the window.

He pulled up to a gas station, and with a clunk, put the nozzle in the car to fuel up. I sat in the passenger seat and looked out at the dark, gray sky. My chest began to squeeze around my heart like a vise. My heart fought to beat against the pressure, fighting for space with my lungs. I struggled to take a breath. I felt like the heavy clouds had collapsed on me. I was smothering in their sooty wisps. The pressure erupted into a single scream that knifed its way out of my throat. Slamming the window with my fists, I tried to break the glass.

Horror flashed across Grandpa's face when he saw me. He hurried to disengage the gas pump and then jumped back into the driver's seat. I turned my shrieks on him as he started the car. He drove away under a barrage of my babbles about being an adulterer, screaming about how much I hated him touching me, and how I was going to go to hell. I screamed, "I told Grandma!"

He slammed on the brakes, leaving black stripes down the middle of the road. I hit the dashboard. "What?" he croaked.

I whispered, "I told her it was the neighbor."

Grandpa eased off the brake and resumed driving at a smooth speed while gazing steadily out the windshield. His mouth formed a run of mind numbing words like a hypnotist. "I'll never do it again. It will be okay. Let me smooth things over with Grandma. You'll see there's nothing to worry about."

My eyes tried to focus on my hands while my head bobbed from the bumps in the road. He told me that he would save money so that I could go to college one day, and then he suggested that we go buy Grandma some of her favorite perfume. Maybe I'd like some perfume too? And I mustn't ever tell the truth of what happened. Never, ever tell.

I don't remember the rest of my stay at their house. I detached from most of my emotions, walking through my days like a sleepwalker. When I flew home, I didn't look out the window on the airplane, even though I had a window seat. I stared at my fold-out tray and felt like nothing in life would interest me again. The lady sitting next to me tried to draw my attention to some of the sites on the ground below, but I didn't respond. She looked at me curiously. I didn't care. When my parents picked me up that afternoon, I told them, "I behaved myself. I had fun. I am tired." I barely found the strength to say that much to them.

My first evening home, there was a show on TV about two boys who had caused their parents an incredible amount of worry by doing drugs. They had been arrested and were serving time in a prison in another country. Mama made me watch it. She shook her head.

"Kids are terrible. You destroy families by your actions and don't even care."

Blood rushed with a roar to my head. I pulled at the collar on my shirt and reminded myself to breathe.

The summer days that followed my visit with Grandparents were some of the worst in my life. My body moved slowly, like it weighed a thousand pounds. It was a struggle to find the energy to wash dishes, get dressed, and brush my teeth. Every bite of food tasted like dust. When I lay in my bed at night, I stared at the ceiling in hopelessness. My life lost its meaning.

While I was outside drifting aimlessly one day, I passed the club house. Instantly, I connected the filthy word 'molestation' to what had happened to me. I fought to control the scream that ripped through my gut, still trying to keep my face placid so that Mama wouldn't suspect anything was wrong.

A few minutes later, she caught me calling to our dog. "Come here. Come here." I growled in my meanest voice. The dog thought she was in trouble and crawled on her belly towards me. As she crawled, a feeling of control infused me, giving me the strength to push down the pain.

"What's going on out here?" Mama's sharp voice cut through the power.

I wilted, ashamed. What am I doing? I've completely lost it. "I'm sorry, sweet doggy," I murmured. My dog wagged her tail in forgiveness and gave my fingers a lick. Mama called the dog inside. "You are the cruelest person I've ever known. Don't you ever touch or talk to the dog again."

About two weeks later, Mama called me into the house. Her voice had a strange twist to it. When I walked inside, she held a letter in a trembling hand. She sat down on one end of the sofa in our living room, and gestured for me to sit on the other side. The hair on the back of my neck stood up. It was the first time she had welcomed me to sit on the sofa with her in the Dark House. She paused for a second to light her cigarette. After taking a deep drag, she asked me what had happened with the neighbor man.

Her words hit like a punch in the gut. Grandma had promised not to tell anyone. I stood up in a fog, my feet directing me to the door before I could stop them. I grabbed my face and pulled, twisting my head from side to side. I couldn't stop this, I couldn't stop it from coming out. A deep, ugly sob escaped. The truth is going to destroy Mama. Like a volcano I exploded.

"It was Grandpa."

She blinked. I stood there frozen. Time didn't move. She suddenly flew up off the couch. I flung my arm up, but she turned the other way. With a violently punch, she slammed her fist into her other hand. "I could string him up by his balls!" She paced up and down the room, clenching her hands and swearing. I didn't know what to think. I had never seen her so angry before when it wasn't directed at me.

Mama paced the living room from end to end.

"Tell me what happened."

The words were slow to come. They had been locked up my entire life. I tried to be honest and shared with her as much as I could dredge up. After about an hour of me starting and stopping, Mama told me she needed time to consider what I had said. She sent me away to my room. Every so often I ran back upstairs to share more memories as they came to me.

That night when Adam came home, she called me back upstairs.

"Tell him," she said, gesturing to him with one of her shoulders. He looked at me with one eyebrow raised.

"So, what's this you've been saying?" he asked.

I was embarrassed and blushed as I retold my story. Mama's questions started to sound skeptical. The final nail in the coffin of her support was when I said, "One last thing, _____ did it to me too." The air felt leaden as they both stared at me with looks of disgust. She leapt to her feet and ran to her room. I heard her lock the door. Adam shrugged and scratched his head. I felt like a ball of yarn that had been pulled apart and was hopelessly unraveled. I scooped up the emotional mess of my confession and stumbled downstairs to my dark basement room.

That night I lured the cat near through the stairway door that was left opened. When he came close, I snatched him up and carried him into my room for a few hours. I dreaded being caught by Mama, but I was desperate. I smoothed down his fur and stroked his ears until he purred. I buried my face into his soft side and my tears made wet patches on his coat. The cat found something he liked and began to lick my hand non-stop. His scratching tongue made a red patch on my skin that gave me something to focus on besides the pain that was tearing me inside.

When I had pressed my luck long enough, I snuck him back upstairs.

The next morning, I lay in bed in disbelief and blankly stared up at my empty bookshelf. Did yesterday actually happen? Oh God! What did I do? The house was quiet when I tiptoed up the stairs. I was too jittery with nervousness and dread to eat breakfast. Mama was still locked in her room, and the house felt cold and empty.

I heard the echo of a hammer and ran to the lattice covered window. Adam was out there fixing the fence at the bottom of the property. I slipped out the door, trying not to disturb Mama, and ran down the hill to where he was.

He didn't look up, but continued to hammer when I came up to him. I waited for him to acknowledge me. Silence. After a minute, I cleared my throat and attempted to break the ice.

"So, I slept well last night."

His hammering slowed, and after the last stroke, he brought it to his side. He tipped his head back and looked at me through the bottom of his glasses. "You're kidding. How could you?" His voice sounded like ice. He turned away and hammered on the fence again.

Chills ran through me as I realized all my fears were true. I was like those boys in the television show, I had destroyed the family. I ran up the hill and hid behind the shed, wanting to go into my room and pull the covers over my head and disappear forever. But, it was daytime, and I wasn't allowed back inside.

That evening Mama drifted out of her room. She had taken something, and her voice was numb. Mama gave me a spacy look. "I don't believe you. You can't even keep your story straight. Besides, if anything happened it's your fault anyway. You seduced him by not staying away from him. I told you before to stay away from him, when you came to me as a little girl and told me what Grandpa asked you to do." She waved her hand impassively at me, when my mouth opened in shock. "You just keep quiet. Don't bother trying to defend yourself. This is your fault. I've dealt with it, and I never want to hear another word about it. From now on it's a dead subject. Now get out of my sight."

I was floored. I didn't know what to say in response to defend myself anyway.

About an hour later, Mama called her Dad and informed him that she had decided not to press charges. "Press charges! I never did anything!" He yelled. That was how Grandma found out that it wasn't their neighbor who had harmed me.

After Mama hung up the phone with Grandpa, her boldness deflated, and she looked like she aged ten years. With heavy steps, she dragged herself to her room and locked the door again, this time staying in her room three weeks.

My stepdad stood outside the door every once in a while, holding cups of coffee and soup. He softly pleaded with her to open the door. As the days progressed, sometimes the food was permitted in, but she never came out.

Finally Mama did leave the bedroom. She walked up to me and said, "I never want it brought up again. It's a dead subject."

I would never talk about it with her again.

She resumed life as though nothing had happened. Her timing was impeccable. I had just received my tickets in the mail, and in just a few days I would be flying out again to visit my Dad in Pennsylvania.

The night before I was to leave I packed my suitcase. Mama came down the stairs and stood in the doorway to watch me. Cigarette smoke swirled around her head, while she studied me. I couldn't meet her eyes. After a minute, she said, "Do not tell him. He'll take you away from us. He'll abuse you like he abused me."

I nodded. I would never betray Mama.

The next day before the sun rose, Mama and Adam dropped me off at the airport terminal. I raced to find my gate, my suitcase bumping into my legs. The flight attendant smiled and winked her eye as I ran on the plane.

The airplane began to move down the runway for takeoff. I leaned my head back into the seat, not able to comprehend how much my life had changed since my last airplane ride. I couldn't think too deeply about it, I had to live another lie for Mama. You can do it. Happy face time! When the flight attendant came by to hand me a pair of plastic wings, I gave her a big smile and said, "Oh thank you so much! Yes, I am flying alone! I am so excited!"

I clutched the armrests with my eyes closed when the plane landed. I almost landed in someone's lap trying to get my luggage down, but friendly hands caught my shoulders. I smiled with gratitude at the man and stepped off the plane. Taking a few deep breaths, I looked about the terminal. This time I spotted Dad right away. His hair was combed in a high wave to one side, and he wore a suit. He threw one hand up in greeting, his other one tucked around his new wife. While he introduced us, I gave her a quick look-over. She was petite, with dark, short hair flipped back over her ears like two shiny bird wings. She pulled nervously at her green cardigan that was buttoned clear to her neck. Her eyes were on Dad as he introduced her, and then she smiled and gently shook my hand.

"I'm so glad to finally meet you! How's your summer been?"

I imitated her grin and answered, "It's been a great summer. I'm so excited to be here!"

It took a few minutes to exit the airport and find Dad's car. "What do you think of this baby, eh?" He said as he threw my suitcase in the trunk. It was a Cadillac with plush blue seats. I ran my hands against the velvety grain and made a dark stripe in the fibers. We pulled out on the highway. Dad called over his shoulder, "We're going to make a few stops before we head home."

They took me out to dinner at a Mexican restaurant. I was surprised to see money at the bottom of a bubbling fountain that stood in the center of the restaurant. Dad told me it was for wishes.

Over enchiladas, he told me about his new job.

"I'm an important person at my new job, CeeCee."

I looked up with the fork half-way to my mouth. I didn't know what to say. He was waiting, so I said, "Oh, good job, Dad."

He nodded and continued. "People have to watch their p's and q's around me. What I say goes. I make good money now!"

After dinner, we stopped at a video store. "Pick out a movie," Dad said. I didn't know anything about movies, so I asked him to pick. He picked out Animal House. That night I cringed with embarrassment every time he gave a raucous laugh.

They lived in a split level house, with my bedroom located across the hall from theirs. My stepmom showed me the bathroom and shyly pointed out the special shampoos and scented soap that she had bought for me. "I hope you like them," she said, her nervous hands wringing a hand towel that she had been folding.

"Oh, they're my favorite!" I said, pretending that I was used to such things.

It was a fancy bathroom, with heat lamps in the ceiling and thick luxurious towels to wrap up in. I was nervous climbing into my first shower. After turning on the water, my hand hovered over the shower switch for a moment. I hope I do this right. I flipped up the shower nozzle and instantly hot water sprayed my face. Sputtering, I jumped back, slipping a little on the porcelain. I rubbed my eyes. What the heck? I eased myself in again, smiling at the wonderful feeling of the hot water. I reached for the orange bottle and squirted some shampoo in my hand. There's nothing to this.

Just then, I saw the water puddling outside of the tub. Ahhhhh! The shower curtain rings clinked as I rearrange the plastic liner. There was hammering out in the hall. I leapt out of the shower with soap still in my hair and stared at the door. Shivering, I held my breath and listened.

No one burst in; no threats were screamed through the closed bathroom door. There was no sound at all, except my pounding heart beat and the running shower.

It didn't take me long to enjoy feeling pampered like I was at a lavish spa. The soaps and shampoos smelled blissful and lathered so easy. After my shower I stood in front of the steamy mirror wrapped head to toe in thick towels, with another in my hair, and spoke to my reflection with my pinky out like I thought a princess might talk.

"Daahhhhhling…..I ahhhhbsolutely must have the honeysuckle lotion for my toes…"

I leaned in closer to the mirror, what the? There was a scar on my face. I had never seen it before, but there it was, stretching like an open mouth along my jaw line. I tried to rub it away with my fingers, thinking it was a bruise or a shadow. I couldn't believe it was there.

Quickly, I got dressed and ran out to the living room to find Dad. "Dad! Look at what I found!"

He glanced at the scar and said, "Oh yeah, you never heard about that? I was changing you when you were a newborn on the counter at our friend's house. Someone left an iron plugged in there. You just rolled over and hugged it to your chest. Third degree burns down both your arms and your face. Hospital kept you for two weeks, and there was a bunch of crap with CPS trying to investigate us. I'll tell you this, the nurses said we weren't fit to take care of you, but they were the ones who gave you a diaper rash."

My eyes grew wide as he talked. Dad nodded and said, "I can't believe you never heard that story. You and I were buds when you were born." He looked at me like he expected the bond to still be there. I gave a half smile and went back to collect my stuff from the bathroom.

Dad and my stepmom left for work every day. They didn't care what I did while they were gone, and I was giddy with all of the choices I had for my free time. Dad had given me the entire series of All Creatures Great and Small. I scrunched into the corner of the leather couch with a bowl of blueberries and read them, one after the other. The sentimental animal stories brought a genuine smile.

In the afternoon, I watched T.V. with the freedom to turn the channels for the first time. Settling back on the couch, I watched Judge Judy and ate fruit rollups. I shook my head and giggled at the ridiculous arguments, the fruit roll-up hanging out of my mouth like a green tongue. It wasn't long before the floor was littered with the long wax-papered curls.

There were no restrictions with the food. I helped myself to grapes, granola bars, and yogurt. I was never hungry during those two weeks.

On the weekend, Dad took me to the mall and bought me bags of new clothes for school. We visited a jewelry department where Dad bought me my first watch and a beautiful pair of gold earrings.

"Ya like them?" he asked. I could only nod and stare at them in the mirror. He took me to a shoe store where the salesman measured my foot for the first time, and I walked out in a pair of expensive tennis shoes. I loved those shoes, and wore them until they fell apart.

Mama called me every day while I was in Pennsylvania. She sounded supportive on the phone, her voice soft, "Oh, it must be so hard on you to be with your awful Dad. How is his anger problem? Has he hit you yet? It scares me honey, to know what he might do to you while you are there, and I am so far away. Are you ok?"

Tears ran down my face. I sniffed and clutched the phone to my head until the ear piece dug into my ear, craving her sweet words. After the previous month of her silent treatment, my body went weak with relief to hear her voice.

"Yes! Oh Mama, it's so hard to be here!"

Dad pulled up in the driveway, so I hung up the phone. He pounded up the steps, his finger pulling his tie lose from his neck. "Did you finish your math work today?" he asked. I gulped hard and shook my head. I had forgotten he wanted to check over the math problems he had given me that morning. His face flushed red. He went over to the liqueur cupboard and pulled out a bottle. "What are you, a Moron?" He shook his head and went to the kitchen for ice.

His loud voice ripped at the fearful memories I had of standing in the corner. Even though he could be kind, he was still a scary stranger to me. Mama was all that I wanted.

When the vacation ended, Dad and my stepmom both hugged me before I was dropped off at the airport terminal. Their arms squeezed tight around me, but we were all pretending. They didn't know the real me, they only knew plastic CeeCee. My life was a secret, and they could never know more.

During the airplane ride home I considered the different phone calls I had with Mama. I felt nauseous. At the end of the plane ride I would find out if Mama accepted me again. When I exited the plane down the stairs, I hesitated for a moment at the bottom and stared up at the starry sky. I didn't want to know.

The artificial lights and stale air gave me an instant headache when I walked into the terminal. Through the milling passengers I saw Adam's arm shoot up. With my plastic smile firmly in place, I ran over. I put my arms around Mama, barely touching her to give her an air hug. She stiffened, but had a smile on her face. The car ride home was silent except for their usual small talk in the front seat. I looked out the window and thought about the prize I had brought home for Mama. She would love it.

We drove down the long driveway again, and the house stared at me with its dark, barred eyes, looking the same as it had the first night I had seen it. Adam brought in my luggage and set it down in the living room. I couldn't wait any longer and unzipped my suitcase right where he left it. As I was digging through my packed clothing, I heard Adam and Mama start to giggle. When I turned back with her prize in my hands, they were both pointing at me with smiles on their faces. Mama stopped laughing and twisted her face into an exaggerated look of disgust.

She snorted, "Wow! What did you eat in Pennsylvania? You're a real little Porker! You've turned into a fat butter ball. I can't believe how round your butt is."

She mimed me by blowing out her cheeks, and held her arms out like a beach ball as she waddled a few steps. Still laughing, she took her gift from me and glanced at it before setting it on the side table.

I knew how Mama hated fat people from the years of disparaging remarks she had made. It was true, I had gained a few pounds, but I was still underweight. Heat filled my cheeks. I wanted to run and hide from their pointing fingers and mean laughter.

She didn't speak to me again after that night. As the weeks went by she kept up the relentless silent treatment. She would never forgive my secret. There was nothing I could do to fix it. I wondered how much worse it would get, but could never have prepared for the change that was coming right around the corner.

~ 17 ~
TWO UNEXPECTED HOMES

Summer was over, although the hot days continued into September. I was caught between a tailspin of emotions that I tried to bury, and school days, where my friends complained about mundane things such as small allowances and boring summer vacation trips. Life at home was different now, because all the torturous punishments had ended. Mama was still ignoring me and even had detached from that horrible connection with me. The first night back from Dad's house I had stood hesitant in the kitchen holding my empty plate while they stepped around me, wondering if I was even allowed to eat.

She no longer watched me with suspicion, and there were no longer lists of things that I had done wrong waiting for me. There were no doors being pounded on. She acted as though she didn't have a care in the world and seemed extra jovial and out-going with my stepdad. Her laughter rang through the house while her eyes looked right through me.

Meanwhile, my emotions churned inside of me, bloated and toxic. But I tamped them all down and pretended everything was okay. I had the strength to do that because of my immense relief that Grandpa would never, ever touch me again.

September brought cooler weather and colored leaves blowing behind the school bus on my way to eighth grade. School was my sanctuary, a place where I could escape to be around people who saw and talked to me. The new wardrobe Dad had purchased helped with my confidence. For the first time in my life, I felt a little bit cute.

I took cross country running for my physical education class that year. Every day Amy and I spurred each other on to run a little farther. "Come on, just to that horse's pasture and then we'll walk. You can do it!"

On this particular day my friend said, "You're so fast. Why don't you try out for the track team? It's awesome! You'd love it."

My lungs were on fire from the two mile run, but there was a feeling of elation that made me feel like I could run forever. I imagined running on the team, the instant camaraderie and the challenge. Mama's face overshadowed the picture; there was no way she would pick me up after practice. I shook my head, "Naw, I have too much homework to ever have time for a sport."

As the autumn months bled into one another, I earned the best grades I ever had in my classes. The principal read the names on the honor roll over the loud speaker during first period. I blushed and picked at my fingernail when I heard mine.

Christmas was a few weeks away, and the dreaded semester finals weighed everyone down. My science teacher stood in front of the class with a text book in her hands, reviewing for the final in an endless drone. She was interrupted by an office aide opening the classroom door and handing her a pink slip. The teacher glanced at it for a moment and called out my name.

"CeeCee, gather your things together and head down to the Principal's office."

My skin felt clammy as I stood up. It felt like I was moving underwater trying to shove all my books and papers into my backpack. Students turned in their seats to look at me. I heard whispers, "ooooh, what did she do?" The teacher rapped on the desk with her knuckles and said, "All right! Quiet down now." I followed the aide out of the room.

As I hurried after the aide I asked, "Hey, do you know what they want?"

She shook her head no and quickened her steps. We walked past the cafeteria, and the smell of spaghetti wafted passed me, making my stomach growl.

I followed her around the corner and walked right smack into my parents. I actually let out a gasp and grabbed the wall for balance. It was surreal to see Mama there, staring straight into my eyes with a solemn expression on her face, as if she hadn't been treating me like I was a ghost for months. She looked so foreign. School was a place where my parents didn't belong, a place that was mine, where I didn't have to worry about them.

Mama cleared her throat and gave a quick glance over at the Principal before looking down at the floor.

Adam told me, "Need to take you to the Police Department, CeeCee."

The bell rang with a raucous clatter announcing the end of class. I jumped at the sound, my eyes darting at the students crowding near us. I suddenly was desperate for privacy as I struggled to comprehend what Adam had said. The Police Department? Was this still about the stolen mail?

During the car ride, Mama spoke from the front seat. "Ok, so during the time I was in my room I called a counselor. I thought she'd help me, but instead the counselor told me that she had to report what I said to the police. I couldn't believe it. Some confidentiality. So it's because of her do-gooder nosiness that we have to do this." Then she turned around in her seat to look at me, "You need to be careful what you say. Maybe only tell them about the dirty magazines."

I wanted to throw-up, caught in a nightmare that wouldn't end. Did I not already tell my secret? It didn't go so well the first time I told it.

Adam parked across the street from a tall building, and we got out. I paused on the doorsteps for a few heartbeats, as Adam waited with the door held open. The steel doors looked powerful, like they were going to lock together and not let me back out. I tried to sift through my story while I stood there. What parts were safe to tell? What parts were supposed to stay a secret?

In the background, little kids were being let out for recess at a distant school. I heard the bell, and screams of, "Tag! You're It!" A lump grew in my throat.

A dark haired woman in her late twenties met us at the entryway. She spoke with my parents for a second and then walked over and laid her hand on my arm. The roar in my ears reminded me to slow my breathing. With her hand still on my arm, the social worker separated me from my parents and led me down a long hall lined with metal doors shut tight on either side. Glaring overhead florescent lights reflected off of the yellow hallway walls reminded me of the prison scene in the TV movie. The beige carpet had a red stripe down the center like a red arrow. I felt sick, wondering what it pointed to.

She opened one of the doors on the left with a metallic click and guided me into a cold, little room. I looked around, and the first thing I noticed was the large mirror on one wall. There was a camera up in one of the corners with a blinking red light. It pointed down to a Formica table with two metal chairs. Behind the table I saw a shelf where boy and girl dolls leaned lopsided against one another.

She gestured to one of the chairs. We both sat down at the table, and then my curiosity got the best of me.

"Why the dolls?" I motioned.

"Oh that's to help the younger kids show us what happened." she answered.

The social worker folded her hands in front of her on the table and in a calm voice said, "Why don't you tell me what happened that brought you here today."

I stared up at the camera. She reassured me that our meeting was confidential, and my parents wouldn't find out what I shared with her. "This is a safe place," she said, "Take your time." I took a shaky breath. Can I trust her?

I told her my history the best that I could, but tried to be careful about what I shared, afraid that I might get Mama in trouble. She was patient and had me retell my story over, and over, and over again. We stayed in the cramped room for hours while the camera steadily blinked and recorded my statement. She asked me questions about Mama. I tried to be noncommittal with shrugs. But she pressed me for a "yes" or "no" answer.

By nine o'clock that night I was exhausted. The social worker called for a break to give me a chance to get something to eat. I was drained, as though I had run a marathon and stumbled back out to the lobby to find Mama. I hadn't eaten since breakfast. My body felt weak and unsteady. Mama examined me from her bench, slowly shaking her head as I walked up to her. Her nose wrinkled, and she said with a sneer, "I saw three policemen come out of the room next to yours. They were standing behind the two-way mirror listening to you. They laughed at you while they were eating hamburgers."

"What? Why were they laughing?" My insides shuddered as though I were naked and on display.

"I don't know?" Mama answered in a sarcastic tone, "What did you say?"

The Social Worker retrieved me from my parents after thirty minutes. We walked back down the institutional hallway again. "Did you eat?"

I shook my head no. She rifled through her purse in search of the coins that I heard rattling at the bottom. We stopped at a vending machine, and she bought me a bag of chips.

When we returned to the room, she asked a few gentle, nonthreatening questions about my favorite parts of school. She smiled at my stories, and I felt a wave of relief that maybe this whole ordeal would soon be over. My muscles unknotted in my neck as my guard lowered. Then, out of nowhere, she asked me if I was scared to go home. Alarmed, I tensed up again, and looked down at the scratches in the table to buy some time. My head nodded, even though I was still undecided of what to say. I was shocked and yelled at myself, Stupid! Stupid! Stupid! Why did you do that?

The social worker studied me for a moment with her eyebrows furrowed and folded her hands back on top of the table. "I've heard enough to warrant pulling you from your home. I'm going to place you into foster care."

I covered my face with my hands and cried, fat tears dropping to the table. I didn't know how to make this nightmare end. She put her hand on my shoulder and said, "I am here to help you, CeeCee. Things are going to get better now."

Rubbing the tears off my face, I said, "Am I going to have to tell them I'm not coming home?"

"No, no, of course not," the Social Worker reassured me. She patted my shoulder, and we stood up. She led me out of the building by a different door.

I was surprised by how dark it was when we got outside. The Social Worker walked with rapid steps to her little hatchback car, her shoes making a firm "Clack! Clack!" sound on the asphalt. She leaned over to clear out the passenger seat of books and papers so that I could have a place to sit down. Tipping my head back, I looked up at the sky at the full moon and was surprised to see that the city lights blocked out the stars.

Our drive was slow. Every traffic light turned red when we hit the intersection. She pulled off at a fast food restaurant and bought us both burgers, foregoing the fries after I shook my head. We sat in the idling car in the parking lot to eat them. After all the hours we had spent talking in the little room, we didn't say very much to each other the rest of the drive to the foster home. I felt like a person in exile. I didn't have any of my belongings with me but the clothes I wore. She reassured me that the foster home would have pajamas and a toothbrush for me. She said, "This is a good move for you, CeeCee. Things are going to be better for you now. Change is going to happen, and we are here to make sure that it does happen."

It was late when we arrived at the foster home, and the other foster kids had already gone to bed. The foster mom met us at the door in her pajamas and bathrobe, with one finger on her mouth to tell us to be quiet. The Social Worker waved goodbye to me, "You are in good hands now!"

The foster mom shut the door and turned to me. In a quiet,matter-of-fact tone, "Ok, let me show you where you can sleep." She led me down the hall, whispering to indicate the bathroom as we passed by the door. Once we were in my room she handed me a white t-shirt, some clown striped pajama bottoms, and a tooth brush, before she said good night and shut the door behind her.

Clutching my new clothes, I sunk down to the bed feeling incredibly dazed. My mind felt like it couldn't catch up to my body. My stomach gurgled over the greasy hamburger, while I rubbed my forehead, trying to adjust. This morning I had been gearing up for my finals at school, and now here I was, in a foster home sitting on a bed covered with a scratchy blanket. Guilt wracked through me, and my stomach flip-flopped. What have I done? Did I get my parents in trouble? Why did the police laugh at me? What was going to happen to me now?

Even though I was struggling with crushing guilt and confusion, there was a tiny part of me that jumped up and down in joy at being free from Mama.

The next morning when I woke up there was sunshine in my room. I pulled back the covers and looked at the strange striped pajamas and then rubbed my eyes. I wasn't dreaming. I was in foster care.

There were voices outside my door. With a deep breath, I walked out to meet the rest of the family. They were gathered at the kitchen table eating quietly, just clinks of the silverware against the bowls. I grabbed a bowl from the stack while one kid shifted to make room for me at the table. They said hi, and were nice enough. But we all were guarded, circling our own vulnerabilities with a fake exterior.

After the kids left for school, I stayed at the kitchen table with a bowl of soggy corn flakes while the foster mom filled the dishwasher. I played with a drop of spilt milk, dragging it with my finger into designs on the table and reflected how I was caught between two worlds. There was the normal world where I attended school, and knew what to expect, and this world where I didn't belong to anything or anybody. As hard as I tried, I couldn't imagine what the next step in my life would be.

I saw a new social worker that day, who said nothing meaningful to me to help me. We sat together in a little alcove off of the living room. I was bored while she shuffled through a clipboard filled with papers. Her pencil made a scratching noise as she checked off a list during her talk with me.

I spent the rest of my time wandering around the foster home, trying to keep out of the way of the foster mom. I didn't want to go home, but I missed school. I sat by the Christmas tree and examined the colorful wrapped presents. Even though I knew there were none there for me, I still felt a little pulse of pain when I didn't see my name. Pushing a few gifts to the side, I scooted under the tree and lay down to look up through the branches at the twinkling lights. My mind was spinning a million miles a minute, but Christmas lights gave me my first little smile in a while.

My parents fought with CPS for two weeks. Somehow, they were able to regain custody of me. I was supposed to be in foster care for a month, and the early release led me to believe that my parents were correct; I was a bad kid. I was confused why Mama would even want me back. Years later, I suspected that it was to keep Dad from gaining custody of me. I was still a pawn in her battle for control with him.

Mama flew into her ferocious tirade the moment that I climbed into the back of the car. Her angry words burned me like a caustic acid. "We are going to get that Social Worker fired for believing a selfish kid like you! How could you lie about us this way? I can hardly look at the teacher I work for any more now that she knows CPS took you away. Oh, I told her all about you. I told her you were a liar. I've told anyone that asks that you're an ungrateful kid who exaggerates and causes trouble."

Mama's rebuke was endless, while Adam piped in like her backup singer, "Yeah! Why did you? Huh? How could you?"

I leaned my head against the cold window and watched the snow hit the glass. I visualized the snow sucking me out the window, taking me into the black night and embracing me in its cold windy arms and numbing all my pain. I was shattered. I had thought I had escaped, only to be sucked back into hell again.

After arriving at home I flipped on the light in my gray room. The ghastly yellow glow seemed to ridicule me, "You thought you could escape here?" I'd learned my lesson, there was no hope and there was no help. I was on my own.

I had been home for a few days and just finished my finals, when I had to pack up my suitcase and fly back out again to Pennsylvania. It was time to visit Dad for Christmas. I tried to hide behind my phony happy face again, but almost didn't care enough to fake it this time. I was too emotionally drained and physically exhausted from yo-yoing between the extremes in my life.

Dark and gloomy weather greeted me in Pennsylvania, and the gloom carried over the entire visit. Dad and I were at odds with each other the whole time. At one point Dad became frustrated with me, because I didn't brush my teeth before breakfast. He stayed moody the entire visit.

We went over to his parent's house for to dinner. I felt emotionless when Grandma hugged me. I craved their love and affection, but there was no place left in me to receive it anymore.

Grandma's house was festive with red and green Christmas decorations, but what caught my eye the most that visit was a picture at the end of their hall of Jesus. The painting was of his crucified face, and his eyes followed me no matter where I stood. Jesus looked angry. I stood in front of the picture with a weight in the pit of my stomach and silently pleaded for his forgiveness. Instead, his disappointed eyes followed me when I left my grandparent's house.

I spent most of my visit in the guest room reading The Lord of the Rings that Dad had given me as a gift. When I returned home, there was only more coldness. It felt like winter lived in my soul that year.

The law required that Mama take me to a counselor. They found one in the next town over that they liked. The counselor had told Mama over the phone that her specialty was, "training disobedient children with tough love." She wanted Mama to know that she had not gone to school for counseling and was not licensed.

A few days after I returned from Pennsylvania, Mama brought me down for my first appointment. I walked in to the office which was located downstairs of her split level home. The counselor sat in an office chair behind a maple desk and pointed to the empty chair opposite her with the pencil held in her hand.

She gave me a small smile and said, "So, I hear you are having some trouble at home."

I nodded, uncertain what she wanted from me. I didn't know what the rules were; did I talk about my family life? Were there still secrets?

"So, why do you think you're having trouble getting along with your parents?"

I told her about the time my parents were angry with me when I woke up late for school. My alarm clock had broken. The counselor shrugged at me and replied, "Saying that your alarm clock broke is a lazy excuse. Everyone has an internal clock inside of themselves. You have to tell yourself what time you want to get up."

"Seriously?" I was baffled. I tried to do that every night afterward, but my internal clock never obeyed what I told it to do.

In another one of our sessions I shared how I was worried about the health of Mama, and how I thought her life was hard because she was always stressed.

The counselor laughed and responded, "You're a kid. Quit acting like a grownup. If you'd quit worrying about your mom and started worrying about yourself, maybe you wouldn't get into so much trouble."

I never talked about the sexual abuse, and she never asked.

After the counselor and I met together I waited outside while my parents took their turn. There was no privacy; the counselor revealed everything I had said to her with them. My parents told her that I was trying to play mind games with them.

Mama was back to her after-school list of things I had done wrong, and she shared them with the counselor. Sometimes it was a sock I had missed on the floor, or a pencil left on the table, but most often it was silverware I forgot to put away. Every time she shared the list, my stomach sank. I never understood how I kept screwing up because I had taken exceptional care to make sure that everything was put away.

The counselor gave Mama some ideas for consequences, but Mama took them to a new level. That night she came into my room around one and flipped the light on. I squinted from the sudden light.

Mama glared. "Get up. I found a dirty plate."

I crawled out of bed and staggered up the stairs to the kitchen, where all the dishes were lined up on the counter waiting to be washed again.

It was like that every night. If she found a single cat poop in the cat box then I was out dumping the cat box in the dark, spraying it with the hose, and putting in fresh litter. I had many nights staring bleary eyed out into the dark night washing clean dishes, hoping to hurry back to bed.

Mama still continued to lock her food up in her room and tightly controlled my portions for breakfast, lunch, and dinner. The counselor never knew about the food, but she thought I was disobedient because Mama told her that I tried to sneak food. The counselor convinced my parents to allow me five dollars of my babysitting money to spend on whatever food I wanted.

Mama gave me ten minutes, and I ran through the store throwing cookies, chocolate, and popcorn in my basket. Food persisted in being weird, and now I was learning to binge, but at least I wasn't hungry all the time. I weighed eighty-five pounds, but Mama was horrified at the junk food I was eating. She chanted to warn me, "Fatty, fatty, two by four, can't fit through the bedroom door."

Part of the counselor's tough-love therapy was an unlicensed, militant foster home that handled teenagers with behavior problems. The foster home was filled with kids who were addicted to drugs and out of control. The first time Mama sent me there she had a huge smile on her face, "Oh, you want to try foster care do you? I'll give you foster care."

She drove through an ordinary suburban neighborhood and pulled up to a dumpy gray house. The woman who oversaw the home came to the front door and raised her hand in a silent greeting to Mama, while I pulled out my duffle bag from the back seat. The woman eyed me as I walked up the cracked driveway to the house.

"I'm Mrs. Alice," she said in a very businesslike attitude, "Come inside."

She shut the door firmly behind me and pushed her thick glasses up her nose. I walked into the dark house, noticing that all the curtains were closed. Several faces investigated me from around the living room. Mrs. Alice pointed out her husband, and her two overweight, late teenaged kids. There were other faces that she didn't introduce, and I assumed that they were foster kids like me.

The first night that I was in foster care Mrs. Alice stated her rules, "There will be no talking for the first twenty four hours that you are in my home. It's the rule that all the foster kids have to follow. Stay seated at that table until I give you permission to move."

I sat at the kitchen picnic table with my back to the rest of the family. The rest of the family and foster kids watched Police Academy and ate chips in the living room. I wasn't given dinner and wasn't allowed to leave my bench for the bathroom. It was easy for me to follow the rules. Life had already taught me that resisting only made things worse.

After a few hours of sitting there my eyes started to sting. I thought I'd shut them for a second. My head bobbed. The oldest son came over and slapped the table next to me, and I jerked awake. I looked bleary-eyed at the strange run-down kitchen and for a minute didn't know where I was. I wondered if I was having a nightmare.

The second day was called the day of the impossible chores among us foster kids. Mrs. Alice assigned each one of us a chore, and if the chore was not done to her satisfaction, she gave another impossible chore. One of the girls had to clean the entire bathroom with a tooth brush. My job was to wash all the windows in the house, inside and out, with newspaper and vinegar. Because the chore had to be done to her high standards, I washed each window several times, and it took all day to finish. It was mindless work. I spent the time reminiscing about a book I'd just finished, called The Borrowers, as I pushed the wet newspaper in never ending circles. The vinegar dripped down my arms as I daydreamed about the conversation I would've had with Arrietty if I had discovered her tiny form peeping at me from behind curtain.

I never knew when I would be sent to the foster home. Mama would wait until I rambled through the door after school and tell me to go pack my bags. She'd say she was tired of my chores not being done correctly. One time I was sent there because my parents wanted to visit my grandparents and didn't have a place for me to stay.

The next time that I stayed at the foster home, I was assigned the impossible chore of shoveling the snow off their back deck. Montana winters meant huge amounts of snow, and the snow had reached in frosty drifts to the top of their porch railings. Mrs. Alice wanted to see the bare boards, dried by the sunshine, when I had finished. That day, I imagined that I was at war and had to hurry and dig the trenches for the soldiers who were on their way. I imagined mortars going off and bullets whistling by my head, as I ducked down behind the porch stairs. Hours passed when I finally scraped the last of the slush off the porch. Mrs. Alice nodded her approval and then sent me to her neighbor's house to do the same thing.

I once mowed acres of their tall grass with a rusty lawn mower that continued to die. One of the other foster kids felt sorry for me, and ran over.

"Let me see that stupid thing. What's the matter with it?" He kicked it a few time and then bent down to see if it was filled with gas, while I admired his arm muscles. Somehow, he tinkered with it enough to get the mower working again. Mrs. Alice's son watched the two of us from up in a fruit tree and pelted me with a couple of wormy apples. Mrs. Alice called her son to come inside, and he scrambled down with a moody expression on his face when he passed me. I shivered when he walked by, but he didn't bother me again.

The last time I stayed with Mrs. Alice, I had brought money with me because it was close to Mother's Day. When Mrs. Alice climbed into her car to go to the store I ran out.

"Do you think you could buy a lilac bush while you are out doing your errands? I want to surprise Mama." I never forgot how long ago Mama had loved the purple lilac bush that grew beside the water pump outside our little brown house. She took my money with a nod.

After she left, I walked over to an overgrown, thickly tangled flower bed that stretched twenty by twelve feet wide in front of their house. Mrs. Alice had told me to weed it before she drove away. I looked at it for a few minutes with my arms crossed, wondering how I was going to get the job done since I didn't have tools or gloves. Giving a big sigh, I sat down in the middle of the weeds and twisted the stems around my fingers and yanked. Some of the plants had thorns, and my hands soon were scratched and stained green. Sweat dripped off the end of my nose, and I swore. Most of the weeds snapped off, leaving the roots behind.

Mrs. Alice's daughter came out with a candy bar, and watched me for a few minutes.

"You know," she said with her mouth full of chocolate, "if my mom sees those stubs sticking out of the ground she's going to make you do something else. You better bite them out!"

Standing up to stretch my aching back, I groaned at the hundreds of inch long green stubs that poked up out of the dry ground. I eased back down on my knees and scraped the dirt from one of the stubs with my fingers trying to dig it out, but the ground was too hard. I gave up, and used my teeth to pull out the remaining parts.

Mrs. Alice pulled up several hours later, just as I was finishing up. She nodded at me, "I got your lilac bush."

I stood up, and dusted off my pants with a smile.

"Come over here and help me haul these bags in," she said, leaving the car door open.

I grabbed the last two paper bags off the back seat and brought them into the house. She held a can of soda out to me and said, "Come to the living room and rest for a minute. I thought we might chat."

I followed her into the other room and sat on the worn out couch while she rocked in the rocking chair. "You've been coming here for a while now. I'd like to know a little bit more about you," she said.

It was the first time we had talked together in all the times that I had stayed at her place. I didn't know what she wanted me to say.

Mrs. Alice started the conversation, "Some of my foster kids struggle with drugs. Do you use drugs?"

I shook my head no, and mumbled, "Mama and I have a hard time getting along."

She stared at me for a moment through her thick glasses and rocked. The silence made me feel claustrophobic, so I talked for a little bit about school. She didn't say anything, just let me babble away. I didn't share much about my home life, but let a few details slip about Grandpa's sexual abuse. I surprised myself when I heard the words tumbling out of my mouth, but the words brought relief, and once I started, I couldn't stop. When the words petered out,

Mrs. Alice had silvery tracks on her cheeks. She beckoned me to sit in her lap while she hugged and rocked me.

I never returned to Mrs. Alice's house again, or to my counselor either. I never learned why.

A week after I returned from foster care, Mama said, "You can invite a few of your close friends over for your fourteenth birthday." I was excited and nervous for my friends to come over. We chattered nonstop on the school bus after school and trooped up the street.

I felt feverish when we walked into the living room. It was strange being upstairs in my parent's half of the house with my friends. Mama stayed out of sight while I opened my presents. She brought out the cake and set it before me and everyone sang. She waited until I had the knife in the cake, cutting the first row, when she said, "CeeCee is irresponsible and selfish. She didn't pick up the dog poop for her guests. She'll have to do it now."

I pulled the knife out of the little blue flower I had been cutting and set it on a plate. My friends looked at me with uneasy frowns, unsure of what to do. I got up and headed outside, and my friends trailed behind me as I trudged from pile to pile with my shovel.

Soon after my birthday, Mama hit me with the belt for the last time. She raised her arm and thrashed me with all of her strength again and again. I was determined to hold back the screams and ground my teeth together from the effort. I would not give in, not ever. Her arm grew tired from beating me and still she couldn't get me to scream. Her face turned red from anger. She marched back upstairs, slamming the basement door closed.

I stood up from my cramped position, with bright red whip marks all over my body, and looked at myself in the mirror. I said to my reflection, "You are strong. You are a survivor. You can survive this."

~ 18 ~
THREE HOUSES AND A POND

My grandparents moved to Idaho, and soon after Mama said she was ready for another fresh start. We packed everything up again and the dark house was put on the market. The house was filled with chaos as Mama and Adam took several trips to scavenge empty boxes from the grocery stores. We spent the next few weeks bumping into towers of boxes, packing, and then unpacking them to find the stuff we needed.

The house sold almost immediately. Mama found a storage unit to hold most of our belongings and furniture. Adam sent out his resume, and we waited on pins and needles each week for news that he had found a job.

In the meantime, I settled into the new rental home. My bedroom was in another converted porch, lined with white house siding on the interior wall. It had two huge windows in the corner that filled my room with daylight for the first time in five years. I loved it. I didn't care about the small room size, or the bugs, or the paint that peeled off the walls and showered on the carpet in white flecks. Every morning, sunshine splashed across my face and made me smile before I was fully awake. This summer felt magical. It was a gift, and it resonated within every inch of me that it was going to be special.

For my fifteenth birthday, my parents gave me a used red manual typewriter. I sat on the floor in the sunshine and typed every day. The keys made a lovely clicking sound, and the bell rang at the end of the margin when it was time to return the carriage, as I filled page after page with my stories and poetry. I entered one of my poems into the local newspaper poetry contest, and it won first place. I saved the newspaper in the same box where I kept the cards Grandma and Dad had sent me through the years.

Every day I still had to stay outside, but now there was a new world to explore. The woods stretched for acres behind my house and spilled out into to a wild strawberry field. The strawberries that grew there were no bigger than my pinky fingernail. I chuckled whenever I found a cluster of them hidden under green leaves. It was quiet in the field, away from all signs of humanity. I'd stretch out on the grassy bed and stare at the cloud animals in the sky. My imagination had free reign, and I drank in its innocence. Spending time in my sweet, secret place slowly recharged my joy for life.

When I wasn't in the strawberry field, I was out exploring the mountain roads that wound around our new house. I walked for hours and hours on the dirt roads and daydreamed that Jesus was walking along beside me. In my daydream, I'd look up at him and say, "I have no idea where I am, or where I am going, but isn't this cool?" And I sensed that he kept me safe and led me home after each adventure.

One time, when I returned home from my secret place, Mama was on the couch with a pile of used tissues all around her. Her eyes were red and puffy from crying. She looked at me when I walked in.

"The cat's gone," she said, before making a low moan. She jumped up to hide in her room.

Three days later, her cat was still missing when I left for my babysitting job. My heart was heavy because Mama was still hiding out in her room. In the back of my mind I always worried about her health. I put the children to bed and threw myself on the sofa. The worry was driving me crazy. We have to find the cat. Mama has to be ok.

I couldn't let myself think about what would happen to Mama if we didn't find the cat. Three days! Where the heck could he be? I slid off the couch and onto my knees in their living room, crying in silence.

"Please God! Please let us find him!"

Real pain started to wash over me as the fear told me Mama was not going to be ok. I started begging God for help, my face scrunched into the couch cushion to muffle my words.

Same as last time, that strange peace came over me again, comforting with its heavy warmth. I couldn't believe it, and didn't want to move in case it went away. I sat there with my eyes closed and soaked in the wonderful reassurance.

The phone rang a few minutes later. It was Mama, shouting through the receiver in amazement, "We found the cat! He was locked in the closet in our bedroom."

I hung up the phone with a smile. The closet in their room had never been opened because Mama wasn't given the key by the owner when they signed the lease. She said she had been lying on her bed when she heard the cat meow. Adam broke down the door to discover the cat curled up inside an old dusty box.

With the cat back, Mama was out of her room once again, but she was acting very strange, like she had a secret.

One morning, a few weeks later, she came out to the kitchen to tell me she wouldn't be there when I came home from school.

"I'm leaving this afternoon to visit someone," she said.

My eyebrows shot up. Why is she being so mysterious? I was still looking at her when she spun around and left the room.

She was gone for several weeks. I breathed in the freedom like it was pure, fresh air.

The first day, I ran the washing machine non-stop cleaning my clothes. I piled all the clean clothes on my bed and jumped into them, wrapping myself in their sweet warmth. Giggles burst out of me. I felt rich to have them all clean at once.

My sheets need to be washed! Jumping up, I tore the sheets and blankets off my bed, and stuffed them cycle by cycle through the washing machine. The blanket Mama had given me, where every stitch was a false 'I love you', melted in the dryer. The nylon fibers stuck together in a gluey mess. I tried to pull the fibers apart, but the yarn stretched and snapped, so I stuffed the mess under my bed.

That night, my stepdad came whistling through the door with a box of ice cream sandwiches in his hand. He handed me one, and we watched TV. It was the first time that I had ice cream sandwiches. I'd never enjoyed a dessert more.

While she was gone, the food cupboard stayed unlocked, and I never got into trouble. My body felt like every part was stretching like after a night of good sleep. It was a glorious summer.

When Mama returned from her vacation, she was still very preoccupied. I caught her mumbling to herself as she wiped the clean counter over and over in never-ending circles.

"No, no. It can't happen. It can't be. Not sure…. When is…. They don't understand."

The house was tense again.

I walked inside one late afternoon, just as Mama hung up the phone. Her hand rested against the receiver for a second, and then she turned and leaned against the counter. She pressed her lips tightly together and stared with blank eyes at her hands. Something was wrong.

I eased up next to her, "Mama, are you ok? What's the matter?"

Clenching the side of the countertop, she whispered, "That was the doctor. The test I took last week turned up positive. They're afraid I have…" her voice cracked. With a few heaving breaths, she said in a voice high like a little girls, "It looks bad." Her shoulders shook with the silent sobs, so I gave her a few awkward pats on her back.

"Is there anything I can do to help you?"

She shook her head no.

"I'm going to go pray, Mama. I'm going to go pray for you right now!"

I ran to my porch bedroom and once again fell to my knees with my head against the side of my mattress. "You've done this before. I need you again. Please make Mama better. She can't be sick. Oh God, please help her!"

I was watching for the heat this time when I prayed. I couldn't help but wonder if it would come again. At the same time, fear told me that Mama was not going to be okay. Not this time. I muffled a sob against my arm.

Tears poured from my eyes when the thick wave of heat rolled over me, so heavy I relaxed against the bed. Every breath felt like I was breathing in a tangible peace that instantly cut off my fear. I lay with my cheek against the bed for at least fifteen minutes, and didn't want to move.

Mama retook the medical test a few days later, and a week after that the phone rang with the good news that it was negative. All was well.

And just like that, it was time to move again. We were going to another rental. I still had boxes packed in the corner of my room.

We moved to the new house in time to start my first year in high school. Because the district was so crowded, they started high school here at tenth grade. I walked down to my new school bus stop with a heavy back pack slung over my shoulder. Chin up, chest out! I told myself, as I walked up to the other waiting teenagers. This is your year!

My favorite class was the yearbook development. I made a friend named Samantha, and we signed up to be on the advertising team together. We spent most of the semester designing the slots and fonts to use when we sold the space.

Finally in late October, Samantha and I along with two other girls were able to skip class and go to town to drum up ads. Hoping to crack my friends up, I dipped my head at the owner of an auto mechanic shop and said, "Ahh Top o' the marnin ter yer dare. Can oi interest yer in buyin' an ad oyt av our auld yearbook?"

Samantha covered her snort of laughter with a cough. The owner blinked, and cocked an eyebrow at me. He shrugged. "Sure."

We ran laughing back to school clutching our checks and advertisement sheets.

When I came home that night, Mama met me at the door. She had a smile on her face. I hesitated, my eyes darted both from the floor to her face and back again. "Here!" Mama said, and thrust a box of instant soup in my hand. I nearly dropped it, before looking back at her, then back at the floor.

"It's for you."

"Thank you Mama!" A huge smile broke across my face. She nodded and walked back to the living room, where her crafts lay strewn across the table.

The rest of the food still stayed locked up with a huge silver lock on the pantry door, but the box of soup stayed out on the counter waiting for me each afternoon.

I couldn't wait to get home the next day to make my soup. There was no snow yet, so I brought my typewriter out by the pond, and sipped my soup as I wrote the stories about the siblings that I had carried in my heart from when I was a little girl.

A flat rock overlooked the shallow pond. When I was done, I lay down on it and gazed into the muddy water. Little tracks decorated the bottom, crisscrossing over the top of each other, made by pill bug larvae dragging their rolled bark tubes. I scooped one out, and its ugly front legs wiggled at me. Yuck! I shuddered and tossed it back in to the water, causing a circle of ripples to expand out across the pond's surface.

The calm continued through Christmas. That year Mama bought me new sheets and a quilt for my Christmas presents. I spent the day lying on top of my bed made with the clean sheets and quilt, and listened to old time Christmas stories on the radio. I twirled a candy cane around in my mouth and wiggled my feet.

God gave me that year as a gift. I was about to enter the biggest trial in my life. The one person that I had always relied on was about to fail me. Myself.

~ 19 ~
FALLING DOWN

Just as tenth grade ended, my stepdad was offered a job in Idaho. They rented a moving truck and we moved two days later, continuing to shadow Mama's parents across the United States. I had to leave most of my belongings behind, including my red typewriter. Mama found a new house in another small, country town. This time my bedroom was in the little addition off of the garage.

As I carried a box off of the moving truck, I bumped into Mama in the kitchen. She twirled a padlock around her finger. Smiling at me, she slid the metallic loop through the pantry cupboard handles and clicked the padlock closed.

"Sneaky girl," she said, wagging her finger under my nose.

Like steam evaporating off a hot road, the lock made the magic from my special summer drift away. Along with it went the last of my desire to please Mama. The hollow spot gave its first booming echo in a long time, its center glowing in a red haze of anger. It fumed out of my mouth, and I answered back. "I'm not sneaky!"

She raised the back of her hand and cracked me across the face. I ran to my room. Mama followed me to the washer and dryer outside my door. I overheard her muttering as she threw the laundry in the machine, "I wish I'd never had her."

From my bed I called, the red haze still driving me, "What Mama?"

She slammed the washing machine lid down. "You just think you're so big and bad. I should have beaten you more when you were younger." The red haze shielded me from caring about her cruel words.

I stood up and headed back to the truck. On my way back through the kitchen I slid a cigarette from a pack sitting open on the counter. I hurried behind the garage and lit it, amazed at how the quick drags filled my body with surges of power.

From then on, I snuck cigarettes whenever possible; trying to catch that same feeling the little rebellious act gave me. Adam caught me one day, when he walked around the corner where I was taking furtive drags off of a long butt I'd found. But, he thought it was funny, so I smoked even more.

Now that I was sixteen I didn't stay outside when my parents were gone on the weekends. I didn't know or care if they checked anymore on me, and ran through the back door as soon as the car left the driveway. I ate frozen cool whip out of the freezer and danced to the Bangles in my bedroom, my hands thrusting out in an attempt to walk like an Egyptian across the floor. When the car returned, I casually slipped back out the garage door.

I needed money to buy cigarettes and new clothes, so I got a job at the local fast food restaurant. Mama drove me a few times before we got into an argument about something stupid. She ended the argument by saying, "You think you're such a tough girl? Find your own way to work and back. And don't you bother other people for rides. Figure it out by yourself."

So I walked. It was a little over eight miles there, but independence coursed through me with every step. Finally, I felt in control of my destiny.

One dark morning, my friend's dad pulled up beside me on his way to work and rolled down the window.

"What are you doing out here? Get in the car." He shifted the car in gear and said, "Your parents are okay with you walking all this way in the dark?" He didn't respond when I nodded.

I became friends with the retired next door neighbor, Mr. Kent. His house was shielded from my parents by a huge hedge of trees. I'd sneak over there after school when Mama told me to go outside. He told me stories from his time in the military while I twirled in a battered swivel chair, eating out of a can of mixed nuts.

One day, out of the blue, he said with exaggerated casualness, "I have this bike just sitting out there, never use it." And he gestured with his pipe out the front door. "It's an old thing, maybe you want to use it back and forth to work?"

I went to the door, arching my eyebrow back at him when I saw the brand new black ten-speed leaning against the wall. Mr. Kent gave a puff on his pipe and stared back at me, daring me to comment.

I laughed. "Thanks. I'll use it when I can." I had to be careful not to be caught by my parents on the bike.

I borrowed it without a hitch for a few weeks. One afternoon, when I was over there to return the bike, Mr. Kent met me at the door.

"Well young lady, care to take a little drive with me while I drop this off at my friend's?" He held a heavy bag of canned food. I didn't have anything better to do, so I nodded. We drove up to his friend's house in the next town over.

She was also retired and lived in a run-down trailer. The driveway was filled with tall grass that hadn't held a parked car in years. He pulled up into the driveway, flattening the grass out before the front of the car, and then pulled the emergency brake.

After clearing his throat, he said in a low voice, "I know things are rough for you at home. Just so you know, if you ever need a place to stay, you can stay here, with my friend. She's a good egg."

I was shocked that he suspected how terrible my home-life was. I couldn't even nod to let him know that I'd heard what he had said. We climbed out of the car without looking at each other and walked to the trailer. His friend welcomed me with a big hug, as though she had always known me.

The walls in her house were lined with boxes, stacks of magazines and newspapers, with the living room chairs and a couch squeezed in among them. There were teapots, fishing poles and baskets hanging from hooks in the ceiling, and glass figurines and dried flowers lining the tops of the cupboards. We sat in the chairs, and I tried to smile through the claustrophobia of being buried under her towering piles.

That night, in my bedroom, I considered the offer. She was a nice lady, although a little eccentric, but I couldn't imagine living there. Besides, she lived too far away from the school and my job down town. But in my heart, I knew I was too afraid to make that break from my parents.

In February, I overheard Mama and Adam plan another visit to her parents. A few hours later, I wiped my sweaty palms on my pants and walked up to Mama in the kitchen. She briskly stirred spaghetti sauce in a pot and gave me a quick glance, before adding some seasoning out of a jar.

I cleared my throat and then the words tumbled out with a rush. "Could you please take me to a counselor? I need to work some things out."

Mama's back stiffened. She held the spoon still for a moment, before giving me the briefest of nods.

She took me to the counselor twice. I appreciate that she did that for me. Both of the days I went it was raining. Mama dropped me off in front of the place, and I'd run in with my hands over my head, finally sitting in the counselors office with my hair dripping down my face.

I didn't go into a lot of detail with the counselor. Instead I focused on my intent to confront my grandfather. The counselor was a brusque, no-nonsense woman.

"Is that what you want to do?" she asked.

I couldn't describe to her how this one thought dominated everything else, as though it were trying to birth itself into reality beyond my choice. I daydreamed about it all the time.

"I have to do it."

She leaned back in her chair with her fingers entwined behind her head and nodded.

During the eight hour drive down to my grandparent's house I flipped through my book to distract myself. My heart rate sped up the closer we got. I could feel my pulse pounding in my neck and wondered if Mama could tell what I planned to do.

We pulled into the driveway. My hands were shaking when I got out of the car so I jammed them into my pockets. My grandparents came out to say hello. I couldn't look at him. After a few minutes I hid in the back bedroom.

The next morning, Mama, Adam, and Grandma left together and abandoned me alone with Grandpa.

I hid in the bedroom, pacing, and tried to work up the courage to say what I planned to say. The words jumbled in my head like buzzing white noise. I tried to swallow. This is a bad idea! Don't say anything. What if he freaks out and everyone finds out I said something? Mama will kill me.

There was a noise in the hallway, slow footsteps. With a whispery sound, he snuck around the corner of the door to my room. As soon as I saw his face, his long nose, and beady eyes, my body started to tremble with adrenaline. Every word that I had prepared vanished from my mind.

He stared at me. Time stopped, as I wavered on the brink of keeping silent forever.

I heard a voice, and it took me a second to realize it was mine. "I can't believe you would do that to me. All those years."

It came out in a shaky burst and wasn't what I planned to say. Still, he was shocked. His hands clenched in front of him while he stuttered excuses that it was no big deal.

"LIAR!" I screamed, and then softer, as the tears started to fall, "You almost destroyed me."

He hung his head. "I'm sorry. I'm so, so sorry." He stumbled out of the room, banging into the wall as he left.

The rest of the visit was very awkward. Grandpa and I stayed in rooms separate from one another, as though physically repelled by an invisible boundary. When he was called into the kitchen by Grandma, I shifted to the living room. When the family joined me in the living room, I escaped out the back door. The other three adults were tireless in their joking and storytelling, their voices and laughter louder than normal. Grandpa and I remained silent. Hearing them act jovial weighed me down.

I wanted to go home.

We left at the end of the week. I looked out the window at the rain falling, and wondered if it was over. Did I do enough to make the pain go away?

It wasn't the last time I would see him. When Easter came that year, it brought more rain, mud slides, and my grandparents. Mama, Adam, and Grandma left for lunch, and Grandpa again stayed behind with me. Once more, he tried to slink back into the bedroom where I was. This time I was stronger. This time, the red haze carried me.

As soon as I saw him I screamed, "What do you think you are doing? You're a disgusting old man! You will never, ever, ever touch me again! I'll scratch your eyes out if you try to touch me! Get away from me! I don't ever want to see you again!"

His face turned beet red and backed out of the room.

Sending him away with his tail between his legs should have empowered me. Instead, as the red haze faded, it left behind the echo that was booming. I felt trapped, and crushed.

I craved control. I started not eating, even when I had the opportunity. If I had to eat, guilt rushed me to the bathroom to purge. The eating disorder soon ruled me, to the point that I even drank water after I purged, to rinse my stomach, and then purged that too.

Mama found out.

It happened one night as we were at a restaurant with my stepdad's family, celebrating my step-grandpa's birthday. I had excused myself to use the bathroom. When I came out of the stall, she was standing there.

"You sick?" she asked.

My heart gave a squeeze. She cares! I wanted to run into her arms and have her hold me. Choking on my tears, I said, "Mama, I have a problem. I can't stop."

She backed away and rolled her eyes. "Well, I'm certainly not going to provide food for you to throw up. You're on your own, kiddo."

She pushed the door open and left. I turned to the mirror. You are such an idiot. Leaning close to the mirror, I tried to clean up the mascara from under my eyes. I fanned my face for a moment, and then walked out.

From that day on, I bought my own groceries. She wouldn't drive me, so the plastic loops of the bag made white creases in my fingers on the two mile trek back home.

About a month later, I came home from the bus stop with a friend. She was complaining about her boyfriend as we walked through the back door. I stopped short with my mouth open, and my friend bumped into my back. All of my belongings were piled up to the ceiling against the interior garage wall.

My clothes were knotted around my shoes, papers wrinkled and piled under books, and speaker wires tangled in blankets. All of my art work and posters had been torn down and piled in with dirty laundry. The drawers from my dresser were dumped and thrown against the wall, my shirts tumbling into the cat box on the floor.

All that was left inside my room was my bed and the skeleton of the dresser. It was sterilized of my existence, a bare prison cell. Mama had even taken my beautiful comforter that she had given me for Christmas and sewed gaudy material over the top.

Mama walked briskly around the corner when she heard the back door open. The smile on her face melted when she saw my friend standing next to me.

Her face was white. "Oh, well, this was a surprise for you. I cleaned your room."

My friend patted me on the shoulder. "Umm, I'll see you tomorrow, okay?"

I didn't notice when she left.

All I could see was my beautiful artwork that I had worked so hard on, now lying torn and bedraggled. Bile rose in my throat, and I almost threw up. Mama had stripped away the identity that I was just learning to express.

I leaned down to pick up one of my cassettes and eyeshadow out of the cat box.

"What? I thought you'd be happy? Your room is always such a pig sty, I couldn't take it anymore!" Mama whirled away with a huff.

The black pit inside of me was breaking apart and spewing its putrid contents. The red haze, panic, grief; all the ugly emotions uncoiled and lashed out with strangling arms. Screaming, I ran into my sterilized room and slammed the door.

I had to stop the pain.

I sat on my bare mattress with heaving gasps and tried to control my breathing. I looked at the wall, the corners of my pictures still taped there from where she had ripped them down. By the door I saw a pink safety razor and lunged for it. There was no hesitation. I sliced my body over and over until railroad tracks ran up my arms and legs. With each bit of violence to my physical body, my mental body became more controlled.

The razor gave me power. I was in control over how much it hurt.

The next day the scabs cracked and oozed whenever I moved my arms or legs. The sharp burns reminded me that I owned this pain.

That night, I skipped my bus after school and went home with a friend. Mama called the police to report me as a runaway. The police showed up at my friend's house, where I hid in their back yard.

I could only stay for a few weeks before I had to leave. They had their own family to take care of. I tried couch hopping at a few different friends' houses, but their parents didn't know I was a runaway. With a sinking feeling I realized there was no place to go. I had to return home.

My parents were stone-faced when I returned. They didn't want me back, but they had no choice. Mama had involved the police. She stood at the door, barring my entrance.

"Are you going to do what I say?"

I nodded.

She continued, "You ever leave here again, you aren't coming back. I assumed the police were taking you to the detention center. I don't want you back, but the police said you're still our legal responsibility."

She looked me up and down, and thumped my chest with her index finger. "You don't like it here, leave. I've always told you when you're eighteen you're out the door. You only have a year left."

I spent as little of time as possible at home, instead, choosing to sit for hours by the river trying to think of a way to permanently escape. I couldn't come up with a plan. The money I made from my job was a pittance.

The weight of depression began to crush me.

I cried every night, when the darkness hid all distractions. Razors no longer helped me cope. I burned myself with cigarettes, hoping the greater physical pain would bring a little relief to my inner core. It didn't work.

Death seemed to be the only option for escape from the pain.

I had only been home a few weeks when I went to a friend's house after work. That night I raided her parent's alcohol cabinet, taking big swigs out of every bottle I found in there, even draining the little bottles I found rolling in the back.

I hoped I might sleep my way into peace. Instead, I woke up the next morning covered in bruises, with my friend sobbing over me.

"You stopped breathing! I was so scared! I prayed for you. I thought you had died. Don't you ever do that to me again!"

She believes in God?

One day Mama found out. She pulled up my sleeve and saw the hundreds of cuts on my arm. She gave her sarcastic laugh and shook her head.

"I'll be checking in all the ditches for your dead body every time I drive to town. I'm going to buy you a blue casket, and bury you with your book of poems and a teddy bear."

I had one dear friend, who I was very close with, try to help me. "Things will get better, CeeCee. My life isn't easy either. I understand," she said, patting my arm.

A week later she dragged me out of the middle of our town's main road, where she found me lying outside her house after a fight with my parents.

"Stop it CeeCee! I can't take it anymore!"

I was ashamed for making her worry, but the guilt of what I was doing to my friend was just one more weight on the heavy load.

One day, I had enough. After work, I went to the little park outside of town. With my back against a tree, I watched the river flow through its grassy banks. The sun was in my eyes, and made me squint. I had a package of straight razors next to me in a paper bag. Pulling one from the package, I looked out at the dark water and cut it deep into my wrist. Then I lay back on the grass and waited, warmth running down my arm, and hoped peace would come soon.

I was found by a couple of drugged out teenagers and carted off to the hospital by ambulance. The Paramedic bandaged my arm. He patted my arm and gave me a half smile.

"What could possibly be so bad?"

The hospital was cold, with bone white walls and floors. The emergency room was teaming with injured people, so they strapped me to a bed until they could attend me, and left my gurney outside in the hall. A woman screamed in the other room from gunshot wounds. The old person next to me had their heart monitor go to a solid flat-line. Tears ran down my face, but I couldn't wipe them with my hands tied to the railing.

They assigned me to a room, first taking away my clothing in case I could hurt myself, and left me makeshift hospital jammies. My arm throbbed under the gauze.

My second night there I received a phone call from another friend. I was happy to hear from him, ignoring that his voice had a crack in it.

He had called to tell me that my good friend who had dragged me out of the street had committed suicide.

I threw the phone as far away from me as I could. I couldn't cry, instead, deep guttural moans ripped out of me while I lay on my side, my arms and legs wrapped around a pillow. I rocked back and forth, back and forth.

"No!No!No!No!No!No!No!No!"

When the psychiatrist came by on his rounds later, I couldn't look up from my pillow.

"So," he said, "How are you doing this evening?"

"Just give me whatever drugs it takes to make the pain go away."

He glanced down at his chart and said, "Do you suffer from highs and lows?"

"Sure," I answered, crumpling the tear stained pillow in my hands.

"Hmmm," he answered and walked out. The nurse brought me Lithium that night.

After I was released from the hospital I was court-ordered to continue to see a psychiatrist because of my suicide attempt. The new doctor immediately took me off of the Lithium, shaking his head in surprise that I had been prescribed it.

I asked him, "What can you give me instead to stop the pain?"

He crossed his legs in his leather office chair and said, "Let's talk about why you feel the way you feel."

He wanted me to talk about my past, but I wasn't ready.

A few weeks later, I snuck out of the house again when a friend knocked on my window at midnight. She was frantic to have me come help her with her friend who was suicidal. It was a long, harrowing night, and when I finally returned home there were three police cars sitting out in the driveway.

I couldn't go home. Mama was done with me.

Through word of mouth at school, I found a half-way-house where a few other homeless kids camped out. I stayed there for a while, struggling to combine work and going to school. Life was dark, depressing, and scary. I was surrounded by kids who felt the exact same way. Instead of being a comfort to me, being around like-minded people fed the depression roaring inside of me.

One day, I was offered the chance to move into an apartment with three complete strangers. They had needed a fourth roommate to be able to continue to pay the rent on the apartment. That opportunity changed my life forever.

~ 20 ~
THE YELLOW APARTMENT

I moved into the apartment two months shy of my eighteenth birthday. There wasn't a spare room available, so I shoved my bed against the back living room wall and jammed garbage bags filled with my clothes underneath it. There were three other roommates, all teenagers.

My first night there one of the roommates tapped me on the shoulder.

"You hungry?"

It was Jim. I smiled and nodded.

We hit it off right away. A few days later we started to date.

The four of us were a loud, rowdy group. There was always alcohol around, and I drank whenever I could. Alcohol was the best escape I'd found yet. But, a heavy buzz always brought out my tears. I'd cry in the corner, my defenses down, babbling incoherently, "You don't understand."

I wasn't like everyone else. I didn't belong. Being drunk highlighted that I'd always be on the outside looking in.

When I sobered up I'd rush to apologize to Jim, making every excuse in the book for my behavior. He always told me not to worry about it.

Jim pulled at my heart in ways that no one ever had, but I still didn't trust him. He'd abandon me when he really got to know me.

Every day was a hard acting job, as I tried to continue to be happy. The echoing pain always pulled at me, telling me I didn't deserve him, didn't deserve love. I'd smile anyway, my face cracking under the façade.

I thought about breaking up with him, before he could do it to me. Depression pulled me down. One day, I couldn't take it anymore and needed some relief. I ran to the bathroom and slashed at my ankle with the razor.

Jim knocked on the door.

"CeeCee? You in there?"

I yanked a ream off of the toilet paper, sending the roll spinning.

"Be out in a minute!" I interjected a cheery tone to my answer.

The doorknob rattled.

"Open the door now!"

There was blood everywhere. Red smears all over the floor, toilet, myself.

"Please! Just give me a minute!" My heart pounded and tears ran down my face. I wiped the floor as fast as I could with the toilet paper.

He kicked down the door.

All I could do was hold myself tight and stare at him wide-eyed in horror, the crumpled toilet paper forgotten in my hand. I'm a monster. Now you know.

He looked at me, at the floor, then back at me. He was breathing heavily. In two strides he was next to me, lifting me up, looking me over to find the source of the blood.

Then he held me.

His love was the most beautiful thing I had ever seen.

Later, he bandaged my cuts. He wiped his eyes with his arm and asked me to never intentionally hurt myself again.

I never did.

I cut back on the alcohol, but we still had crazy parties every weekend. It was a Thursday evening two weeks after he caught me in the bathroom. We were lying on the couch drinking beer, when Jim surprised me again.

"You believe in God?"

I nodded.

"You know he loves you more than anything. He loves you more than I love you."

I considered that for a moment. That was a big statement.

"Don't you have to be good? I'm not good." I said, tipping the beer bottle for emphasis.

Jim insisted God loved me anyway. "Just tell him you want him to be your savior."

I definitely needed someone to save me. I became a Christian that night, even though I didn't understand why God would want me.

Jim and I eloped eight weeks later. I stayed up nights questioning myself. What did I do? Was I ready for marriage? Jim would give me a loving look that pulled me back to him again.

The first year of marriage was touch-and-go for me. It shouldn't have worked. We fought weekly over everything, and each time I waited for him to use the "D" word. How could it end in anything but divorce?

There were times that I fought with him, just to push him to see if he'd give up on me. It was hard to reconcile afterwards, because I didn't believe he really forgave me. But Jim did, and I learned to forgive, too. His love for me, wrapped in a human body that still got angry and made mistakes, opened my mind to what love really meant.

My first daughter was born in the middle of my twentieth year, the same hour that I was born. When they put her in my arms I burst into tears, and hugged her sweet, warm body close to me.

I felt like God was saying the broken places inside of me were going to be restored. I smoothed back the little curl on her forehead. My baby will always love me.

A week later she developed colic. She screamed for over fourteen hours every day. The doctor told me that it was a stage my baby had to outgrow, and there was nothing they could do. Sometimes, I wanted to bang my head against the wall with frustration when she screamed nonstop, hour after hour. But, even when everything I tried brought her no relief, I still rocked her in my arms to comfort her. "Mama's here, Mama loves you." I never would have shut her away until her face turned black. She was my treasure.

Soon after she was born I opened the bible at random, hoping for some encouragement. The book of Matthew stared up at me. Like a punch in my stomach, the memory of the adultery scripture hit me. I wanted to thrust the bible away and go flip on the TV. But then, something Jim said came to mind, "There's no condemnation in Christ." My stomach rolled. I took a deep breath and looked down to where my thumb was resting.

In red letters it said, "But if anyone causes one of these little ones who believe in me to sin, it would be better for him to have a large millstone hung around his neck, and to be drowned in the depths of the sea."

In the next instant, I felt God destroy the lie that had connected the adultery scripture in Matthew 5:3 to my memories with Grandpa. A huge weight I hadn't known I was carrying fell off of me. I felt God's reassurance that I had been the victim.

Jim and I began attending a local church every week. One Sunday, I heard the pastor talk about God's love for all of us. What did that mean? When the pastor spoke of God as our father, my wisp of trust in him shrank; fathers were scary. Then the pastor read from the bible, "If you love me you will obey me." I arched my eyebrows. I knew how well that worked with Mama-- a big fat failure. I could only imagine what God would do if I failed him.

But, then I remembered the times I had prayed and felt his comfort. It was confusing.

In the meantime, life went on. Jim and I were blessed with two beautiful daughters, and two wonderful sons. I had to smile to think that God had heard my prayer all those years ago in the club house when I was a little girl.

My children made me feel like the richest person in the world. They taught me so much about myself. I couldn't understand why parenting didn't teach Mama the same things. I couldn't wait until my children were old enough to tell me what their favorite color was, their favorite ice cream, or favorite book. They amazed me. I peppered them with half as many questions during the day as they asked me.

The most important thing for me was that my kids knew I loved them. I wanted them to know they had a voice, and I was there for them even if they thought they were in trouble. God gave me the idea of a "mad bed". When my children needed to get something off their chest, we sat on my bed and I listened – even during the times when everything in me wanted to react. It was an open door policy. And it was a place where I could tell them I was sorry if I learned that I had somehow hurt their feelings.

This tradition forged our family motto – "We're not the perfect family, we're the forgiving family."

Trying to walk in love and trust made the shackles that fear had over me glaringly obvious. I started having anxiety that something bad would happen to one of my loved ones. Nightmarish day-dreams would flash through my mind of my husband getting into a car accident if he was a few minutes late, or my children getting kidnapped, choking, or becoming sick.

Jim told me to talk to God about it, but I was sure I'd be punished for my lack of faith. For some reason, that fear finally made me realize that I had put God in the same place Mama had once held in my life. Mama had punished me for any weakness, and destroyed all hope, happiness, or freedom that I had, so why would I expect God to be any different?

The more I thought about it, the more that I saw how I was locked in a cycle of begging for God's forgiveness, and trying to turn over a new leaf, like I had with Mama.

It didn't end there. I realized the same cycle was being reenacted with my oldest daughter. I didn't trust that my daughter knew that I loved her. Whenever she was angry at me I felt crushed, and saw Mama's face rejecting me. Several times a day, I apologized to her, almost begging her to recognize that I loved her, like I had done with Mama.

In both situations I knew I was acting out of a damaged place. I was desperate to break the cycle. I wanted to learn about healthy love, and have Mama's definition eradicated from my life. I wanted to become whole, but didn't know how.

~ 21~
THE GHOST COMES ALIVE

"Stupid, can't do anything right. Such an idiot. Can't believe you said that! Lazy, so lazy. Everyone else can do it. What's wrong with you?"

I heard it every day. Words my mom once said, words I said to myself. I never let myself off the hook. "You can do it better! You should do more! They think you're an idiot, stupid, stupid lazy."

At the same time I'd tell my kids again and again how precious they were to God. We'd play ring-around-the-rosy, all of us singing at the top of our lungs "Jesus loves me, this I know! For the bible tells me so."

But I still didn't believe it for me.

In many ways I wanted to give up. I didn't see how the puzzle pieces inside of me could ever be put back together. I felt like Humpty Dumpty, doomed to always be broken.

My breakthrough came when I searched out who God said I was in the bible. I needed to know what he thought of me. Did his voice sound like my mom's? When I read the words-- loved, sought after, friend, and accepted—I softened inside. I saw a choice. I decided to quit calling myself names and try to believe I was made for something more. God said I was his daughter, desired and chosen. My fears melted when I realized he was never mad at me. He saw value in me even when I couldn't. My name wasn't Fifth Wheel any longer. He called me his precious Beloved.

As happy as that made me, I could see that wasn't enough; I had to love myself too. To do that, I had to be the advocate for the little girl in me who had been abused. With a chill, I realized that for years I had justified the abuse under the guise of love. I did that, because as an adult, I still tried to have a relationship with Mama. The only way I could reconcile being around her was to pull a "blanket of forgiveness" over my past, and treat it as though it had never had happened.

Now it was time for me to validate all of the emotions that had been denied to me as a child. The forgiveness I'd offered hadn't been real; it was denial. Denying what had happened wasn't going to bring me freedom.

But, it was so hard for me to admit that I had been abused. The memories hurt, and I didn't want to face them all again. It was just too easy to say, "I'm an adult now, the past is over." I sat down to write a letter to Mama, a letter I never planned to send. I could barely get the words on the paper. Family loyalty, the life of secrets, and not wanting to rock the boat of my adult relationship with Mama all held me in an iron grip. I struggled against the brainwashing that had trained me to believe that my past was my fault; I could have been better, or, I was too sensitive. But God showed me that if I didn't see the offense against me, then what exactly was I forgiving?

So, I wrote.

And I cried.

Mama stole my childhood away from me. She beat me, broke me down, starved me, humiliated me, allowed me to suffer sexual abuse, and dehumanized me. But worse of all, Mama withheld her love and affection from me. And by the grace of God, I forgive her.

Grandpa robbed my innocence. Sexual abuse has a shameful stigma. We whisper about it behind closed doors. But I stand up for myself. It wasn't my fault. It has no power anymore to make me hang my head. I forgive him, because it releases me to move forward in life.

It was a hard road back to health. I went to counseling, and had supportive friends and family who helped. But most of all, I needed to believe I was worth a restored life.

Those four steps were huge in my journey to well-being; realizing that God loved me, accepting the truth about what happened to me, allowing myself the emotions the abuse caused, and finally, forgiving those who hurt me. I learned that sometimes I have to forgive even if there is no apology, so that I can be free. Through the years, I've revisited those steps, sometimes for different memories, and sometimes for the same ones I thought I'd already worked through. But isn't getting healthy like an onion? So many layers of the same thing. I tried to be kind to myself, and celebrate the progress.

There were other ways that I grew healthier, but they happened in an organic way through my everyday life. Situations, like when my children became angry with me, would trigger dark feelings of rejection and abandonment. I'd ask myself, "Why am I reacting this way? Is my anger distorting this situation?" If I took the time to search out the root of my emotion, more often than not, it stemmed from a childhood memory. Once I knew the reason behind the way that I felt, my defensiveness lifted away. I could return to listen and respond with a clear head.

Because I cared about my children's troubles, I could see how God cared about my troubles too. I sat on my bed one day, looked up at the ceiling and said, "God, I'm on the mad bed." I don't know why I looked at the ceiling, maybe because I thought of God as being "up there." I poured my heart out to him honest and open, just like my children did with me. I felt his comfort, even as the words tumbled out ugly, angry, and made me feel unlovable.

After that day, I quit trying to be a "good girl" for him. I realized he had never seen me as a bad person whom he chose to love anyway. He saw me as his precious child, just like how I saw my kids.

I still struggled with accepting forgiveness from my family and friends. I was convinced that people wouldn't like me if I wasn't perfect. A friend sat me down once, and said, "CeeCee, we all make mistakes. You make mistakes because you're human, not because you're a monster."

It was hard for me to believe her, but over time I learned that conflict was usually patched up just by taking the time to listen to one another. It was so freeing when I realized I wouldn't be rejected for making a mistake. No one expected me to grovel for forgiveness, especially God.

Another big step towards freedom was when I figured out that my emotions were not truth. Truth was truth, regardless of whether it "felt" true to me or not. The more I treated my emotions as the seasoning of my focus, rather than the meal, the more I experienced what I had longed for my whole life; peace. My peace was this; God had gotten me this far, he was going to get me the rest of the way.

I started feeling comfortable in my own skin. I quit analyzing everything I said and did to see if I could have done it better, and stopped worrying that I would do something to offend Jim or my friends. I chucked the fake smile away forever and let the real me shine forth, come what may.

While raising my sweet family, I wanted my children to have a lot of memories that reaffirmed how valuable they were to me. We played board games, card games, and had snowball fights with marshmallows in the middle of summer. I read hundreds of books out loud while they sipped from cups of hot cocoa and sat sprawled out on pillows on the floor. We chased each other around the house and tickled one another when we were caught. We did tons of crafts. I smiled even when my boys glued their fingers together, or when there was colored marker on the table. I taught them, "Mares Eat Oats," and we sang at the tops of our lungs until it sounded like wild gibberish and laughed and laughed. When they broke one of my special things, I might be mad until I saw their worried faces and then I'd tell them, "You are worth more to me than anything material."

I did things that didn't come natural to me, like when I taught them to bake. Sometimes it felt like a grin-and-bear-with-it moment because of the mess and the slow speed. I silently counted to ten while they stumbled through a cookie recipe, spilling half the flour, as an egg slid off the counter and onto the floor. In the end, my heart burst with joy to see how proud they were to share the cookies they had made with their Dad.

I fixed both of my girl's hair in ribbons and bows, and we played with my makeup. They giggled while they put eye shadow on me and drew on big red lips, and I taught them to kiss butterflies on tissue. One day my little girl ran behind me as I sat in a chair at the computer and began to brush my hair.

"Mommy, your hair is so soft and pretty," she said. "Can I braid it, Mommy? Let me put this ribbon in it and make your hair beautiful."

When I felt my girl's hands gently pin up my hair, I closed my eyes and a tear trickled down my cheek. The sting of that long ago memory of Mama refusing to brush my hair disappeared.

It wasn't long after that day that I realized God had completely healed the dark pit that had echoed inside of me my whole life. There was still some unaccounted time from my childhood, but God had proven that my healing didn't rely on me remembering everything. If the memory was important, somehow I would be reminded.

My Dad died before he and I had a chance to develop an adult relationship. He never knew about my other life, or my secrets. I can't help but be sad at what might have been. I had learned as an adult that he had life-long battles he wasn't able to get free from, and my heart broke. I wish that he could have known happiness.

My mom has no contact with me. It's a broken relationship that I didn't break. I love my mom, and I will love her forever. I deeply want to see love and wholeness restored to her life. I've finally accepted that I can't do anything to make her get healthy. And because God loves me so much, I trust God to take care of her. He's waiting for her to let him heal her broken places. It breaks my heart that I may not be a part of her healing journey, but I am thankful he is.

My restoration has happened cohesively, and it happened in starts and spurts, it happened in a rush, and in fire. It's only when I look back that I can see how the healing thread is entwined so perfectly throughout my life that it could have only happened in that way. Looking forward the thread disappears, but I believe God is still weaving it. I've learned through all my experiences that sometimes breaking new ground to make a healthy life looks messy, but it's still new ground. I'm not afraid of messy, because it's in the messiest of times when I've had nothing left to give that I've sensed God's arms wrapped around me, telling me that I am forever his. He will never leave me nor forsake me. He loves me. He loves me. He loves me. I am an arrow, and I point to God's love. And so, for the rest of my life, that's what I'll point to.

I cherish the healing of each broken area of my life like a mosaic, because I see how the healed scars hold together a picture of beauty culled from the ashes. I was created for love and loved by my Creator. We've walked a long way together.

My Mother's Day Poem

To my darling children,
My reason to smile every day.
Each one of you has confidence in me
And I am humbled by your faith,
You trusted me to be the mom
I never had.
And I learned.

I discovered that a mother's hand is caring.
Where I knew a harsher hand,
You caught mine up for ring around the rosy,
Taught me how a small hand fits into an adult's.
Full of love and safety,
Miss Mary Mack
Tickling silver buttons down the back.

I realized a mother's love never runs
As long as I have breath, I will be there for you.
Agape love-not earned, only values
Not the perfect family, but the forgiving family
Through thick and thin
Welcoming arms
And the door is always open.

I encouraged you to Get up and try again,
You can do this, I have faith in you.
I believe in you.
Speaking from truth, from hope
You four have always made me proud.
You believed in yourselves,
And you inspired me to do the same.

I saw that loving you wouldn't heal the hole in my heart
For a mom to love me.
I could never expect you to fill that empty place.
God showed me that spot wasn't broken forever
He came gently with healing,

His truth and restoration,
And I became the mom that I had once needed.

No mother is perfect.
Sometimes a mother sows what she reaped,
Sometimes we make mistakes.
We let our kids down,
We disappoint them.
God knows,
And He can cover all mistakes.

Today marks my flag on top of the mountain.
I started in a place far from here.
Basking in God's grace and love,
His hope
Celebrating my two Sons and two Daughters-
Thankful for their celebration of me
God's mercy.

I love to hear from my readers! Here are some ways to reach me:

My blog- http://joyfullivingpafterchildabuse.blogspot.com/
Email- ceeceejames777@gmail.com
Facebook- https://www.facebook.com/ghostnomore

ABOUT THE AUTHOR

I love to write, paint with watercolors, and eat chocolate. Not necessarily all at the same time. I love to do pranks too, usually just on my poor husband who luckily puts up with me and lets me think I'm clever. One of my favorite pranks was sewing his work t-shirt neck-hole shut on April Fool's (I made him lasagna that night to make up for it.)

He does a few on me- his last one was hiding an old helium birthday balloon under the covers at night. I had just finished a spooky story, and as the last one awake, I checked the doors and turned off the lights. As I climbed into bed this apparition rose out of the covers, and I screamed....until I heard him laugh.

I still owe him for that one..... ;)

Thank you for reading this, and have a great day!

~CeeCee

Made in the USA
Middletown, DE
16 October 2018